# Bullying

## ISSUES

## Volume 122

**Series Editor**
**Craig Donnellan**

**Assistant Editor**
**Lisa Firth**

**Independence**
Educational Publishers

First published by Independence
PO Box 295
Cambridge CB1 3XP
England

**British Library Cataloguing in Publication Data**
Bullying – (Issues Series)
I. Donnellan, Craig II. Series
302.3'4


ISBN 1 86168 361 8


**Printed in Great Britain**
MWL Print Group Ltd


**Layout by**
Lisa Firth


**Cover**
The illustration on the front cover is by
Angelo Madrid.

# CONTENTS

# Introduction

*Bullying* is the one hundred and twenty-second volume in the **Issues** series. The aim of this series is to offer up-to-date information about important issues in our world.

*Bullying* looks at bullying and young people, the growing problem of cyberbullying and bullying in the workplace.

The information comes from a wide variety of sources and includes:
Government reports and statistics
Newspaper reports and features
Magazine articles and surveys
Website material
Literature from lobby groups
and charitable organisations.

It is hoped that, as you read about the many aspects of the issues explored in this book, you will critically evaluate the information presented. It is important that you decide whether you are being presented with facts or opinions. Does the writer give a biased or an unbiased report? If an opinion is being expressed, do you agree with the writer?

*Bullying* offers a useful starting-point for those who need convenient access to information about the many issues involved. However, it is only a starting-point. Following each article is a URL to the relevant organisation's website, which you may wish to visit for further information.

\*\*\*\*\*

# CHAPTER ONE: BULLYING AND YOUNG PEOPLE

# Bullying

### Information for secondary school pupils

### What is bullying?

Bullying is when people deliberately hurt, harass or intimidate someone else. Every year, more than 20,000 young people call ChildLine about bullying, making it the most common problem we're phoned about. These are some of the ways young people describe bullying:

- being called names;
- being teased;
- being punched, pushed or attacked;
- being forced to hand over money, mobiles or other possessions;
- getting abusive or threatening text messages or emails;
- having rumours spread about them;
- being ignored or left out;
- being attacked because of their religion, gender, sexuality, disability, appearance, ethnicity or race.

### If you are being bullied

*'A girl at school was constantly calling me names. I didn't know what to do, so I called ChildLine. They encouraged me to find an adult I could trust and to tell her how I felt. Talking about it made me feel a lot better, and the teacher I talked to sorted the other girl out.'*
Charlotte, 16

- You shouldn't feel ashamed about being bullied. It's not your fault – but it is important that you get help. No one deserves to be bullied.
- Is there someone who you would feel comfortable talking to about what's going on? Maybe a friend, someone at your school, someone you live with or just someone you trust.
- When you've decided who to talk to, tell them what's happening and how it's making you feel. They might be able to tell you what you can do about it, or can help you decide what you want to do next.

- If you're being bullied at school, ask someone (such as a teacher) to tell you about the school's guidelines on bullying. Most schools have a written policy on bullying, and this may give you an idea of what you can do and what your school should do.
- If you can't think of someone to talk to, you could call ChildLine on 0800 1111 to speak to an adult who is there to listen and help you think about what you can do.
- If you talk to someone about what's happening and it doesn't help, don't give up. Sometimes you may need to talk to more than one person. You have the right to be helped, and don't have to put up with being bullied. Always remember that it is not your fault.
- Trying to remember things accurately can sometimes be difficult, so keep a record of what happens to you. Writing it down is often a good way of being sure about what, when and where things happened.

- It's important to feel safe. Are there ways for you to keep yourself out of harm's way? For instance, you could walk home with friends rather than on your own, or ask someone to stay with you if you feel threatened.

### If you witness bullying

*'I saw a small boy being bullied by a gang in the park. They swore at him and kicked him. I was too scared to do anything in case they turned on me.'*
Duncan, 13

- Don't ignore what happens.
- Let the person who's being bullied know you've seen what's going on and are concerned.
- Encourage them to tell someone.
- If it is in school and you are worried about it, you may need to report the incident. Try to find out who to report bullying to. If you are worried about putting yourself at risk, can you tell someone about the bullying in confidence? Write them a note about what you saw.
- Teachers are often the last to know that bullying is going on.

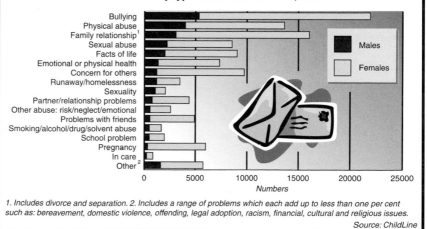

**Calls and letters to ChildLine**

Calls and letters to ChildLine: by type of concern and sex, 2002-2003

Categories (top to bottom): Bullying, Physical abuse, Family relationship[1], Sexual abuse, Facts of life, Emotional or physical health, Concern for others, Runaway/homelessness, Sexuality, Partner/relationship problems, Other abuse: risk/neglect/emotional, Problems with friends, Smoking/alcohol/drug/solvent abuse, School problem, Pregnancy, In care, Other[2]

Legend: ■ Males □ Females

X-axis: 0, 5000, 10000, 15000, 20000, 25000 — Numbers

1. Includes divorce and separation. 2. Includes a range of problems which each add up to less than one per cent such as: bereavement, domestic violence, offending, legal adoption, racism, financial, cultural and religious issues.

*Source: ChildLine*

If they are going to be able to do anything about it, they need to know it's happening.

---

*Bullying is when people deliberately hurt, harass or intimidate someone else. Every year, more than 20,000 young people call ChildLine about bullying*

---

- If there is a problem with bullying in your school you may want to encourage others to get involved in anti-bullying schemes such as poster campaigns or support groups run by pupils. Maybe you could put on a drama presentation to raise awareness in your school.
- Are you aware of your school's anti-bullying policy? Can you think of ways to make it more effective? You may be able to talk to your school council or members of staff.
- If you are concerned about someone who is being bullied or want some more information you can call ChildLine on 0800 1111.

### If you are bullying someone

*'It got to be a habit. The awful thing was that I felt good seeing him cry. The others laughed and that made me feel even better. But then the teacher said that he was in the hospital because he had tried to hurt himself to get away from the bullying. It was only a bit of fun really – I didn't mean him to take it seriously.'*
Jay, 15

- You do have a choice – just because you've bullied others in the past doesn't mean you have to keep doing it!
- People who are bullied can feel upset and scared. You can put a stop to that by changing your behaviour.
- You can get into a lot of trouble if you keep bullying others – you might get suspended or excluded from school or, in extreme cases, the police might get involved.

- Sometimes things happen to you that make you more likely to bully others – being bullied yourself, for instance, or having problems at home. It's important to get help for yourself, rather than taking your frustrations out on others.

Calls to ChildLine are free. You can either call the helpline on 0800 1111 or write to ChildLine, Freepost NATN1111, London E1 6BR. If you live in Scotland, you can also call ChildLine Scotland's bullying line, Monday–Friday 3.30pm–9.30pm on 0800 44 11 11.

Children who are deaf or find using a regular phone difficult can try our textphone service on 0800 400 222.

It can sometimes be difficult to get through to ChildLine when a lot of children are trying to call us, but do keep trying and you will get through to someone who can help.

To read more about bullying, visit the ChildLine website at www.childline.org.uk.

To see how peer support schemes can help your school tackle bullying, visit www.childline.org.uk/schools.asp.

- The above information is reprinted with kind permission from ChildLine. Visit www.childline.org.uk for more information. ChildLine and the NSPCC joining together for children.

© NSPCC

# Are you being bullied by other pupils in school?

---

### Information from ChildLine

We all like to fit in with our own age-group and sometimes we do things or behave in a particular way because we don't want to be left out.

How do you say NO to people when they are putting you under pressure?

This is Sam's story:

'Break time was the worst. This group of girls used to hang around by the seats under the trees. It was out of sight of the school windows and that's why they went there. At first, they were all right and I was new, so was grateful that they let me be part of their group. Then they wanted me to chip in and buy cigarettes. I said I didn't smoke and that's when it started. They got all the other girls in the class to stop talking to me. They just completely blanked me.'

Things got worse for Sam. She got really down about the situation and on her way home one afternoon, she phoned ChildLine.

'It was so good to talk to someone. I thought if I told anyone – teachers or parents – the bullies would just get back at me. Other people had made things worse for themselves when their parents had complained to the school. The counsellor helped me think through some really good stuff. She asked me about people at school I could talk to. I thought of one of the sixth-formers who was really nice to us when we started. I told her about it and said I didn't want a big fuss. She understood and she started coming around the school at break time to send the girls off. She also went to the Head of Year and talked to her without naming anyone.'

If you'd like to know more about how ChildLine can help you, go to www.childline.org.uk.

- The above information is reprinted with kind permission from ChildLine. Visit www.childline.org.uk for more information. ChildLine and the NSPCC joining together for children.

© NSPCC

# Homophobic bullying

## Information from the Anti-Bullying Network

### Is homophobic bullying a problem in schools?

Homophobic bullying has been reported in primary as well as secondary schools. It may be directed at young people of any sexual orientation and at children who have not yet reached puberty. Teachers, parents and other adults in schools may also be bullied in this way.

Homophobic bullying in schools can be a problem in a number of ways:

- children who experience it have their education disrupted. They may be unable to concentrate on lessons because of feelings of fear or anger. Their self-confidence may be damaged and, as a result, they may never fulfil their academic potential;
- it can be a particular problem for teenagers who are confused or unsure about their own developing sexuality. Some victims are driven to the edge of despair or beyond, with lasting consequences for their emotional health and development;
- schools that ignore it, or deny its existence, are not helping young people to develop a concern for the welfare of minorities and tolerance of difference.

### What is homophobic bullying?

Homophobic bullying can involve physical or mental violence by a group or an individual. It is often aimed at someone who has poor defences and who, as a result, may be significantly upset. Victims may be male or female. What distinguishes it from other forms of bullying is the language that is used. Words like 'queer' and 'poof' and 'lezzie' have been used abusively for many years. They have now been joined by words (such as 'gay' and 'lesbian') which were formerly descriptive but which now may be used as general insults. In some youth cultures, 'gay' is now used as a derogatory adjective to describe objects and people that may have no connection whatsoever with homosexuality.

Both boys and girls may be subjected to homophobic abuse.

### Why does it happen?

The root cause may well be prejudice against gay and lesbian people. Even very young children, who do not understand what homosexuality is, may be encouraged to indulge in homophobic behaviour by this general prejudice.

Individual motivations may be more complicated and, as in the case of other forms of bullying, may include a desire for power or a need for affiliation: some people gain satisfaction from imposing their power on others and a group will be strengthened if someone else is outside that group. Identifying people as being different because of their gender orientation may be a convenient excuse for isolating and persecuting them. The bonds that tie the members of a group together are strengthened because the members are not 'different'.

Fear may also be a motivation – as the word 'homophobic' suggests. This can be a fear of the unknown, a fear of someone who is perceived to be different, or a fear which is based on uncertainty about the nature of their own developing sexuality:

'Keep away poofta.'

'Here he comes, backs to the wall.'

Many adolescent boys say that the worst thing anyone can call you is 'gay'. In accusing others of being gay they may seek to demonstrate their own masculinity.

### Who bullies?

Both sexes can be involved in homophobic name-calling. However, anecdotal evidence suggests that boys are most likely to be victimised by other boys. The bullying, especially if it is physical or verbally aggressive, is often deliberate but sometimes bullies may not realise the harm that they are doing. They may believe that their victim enjoys their 'jokes', or that the label they have attached to him is simply a nickname.

Some very young children indulge in homophobic bullying. In one Scottish primary school the head teacher reported that boys as young as seven regularly used words like 'poof' and 'gayboy'.

Teachers are rarely accused of such overt actions but, by the careless use of words such as 'sissy' or by simply failing to challenge homophobic name-calling, they can be perceived as giving tacit approval. One mother described what happened to her nine-year-old son:

'He is a sensitive wee boy who doesn't enjoy sport. On a cold, wet, windy day he was standing shivering on the rugby field when the PE teacher came over to him and said, "If you're just going to stand there shivering, why don't you do what you do best – go and play with the girls".'

- The above text is an extract from information provided by the Anti-Bullying Network and is reprinted with permission. Visit www.antibullying.net for more information.

# What is racist bullying?

## Information from Kidscape

Any hostile or offensive action against people because of their skin colour, cultural or religious background or ethnic origin.

It can include:

- physical, verbal or emotional bullying;
- insulting or degrading comments, name-calling, gestures, taunts, insults or 'jokes';
- offensive graffiti;
- humiliating, excluding, tormenting, ridiculing or threatening;
- making fun of the customs, music, accent or dress of anyone from a different culture;
- refusal to work with or cooperate with others because they are from a different culture.

*The Race Relations Act 1976 states that schools and governing bodies have a duty to ensure that students do not face any form of racial discrimination*

### Legal position

The Race Relations Act 1976 states that schools and governing bodies have a duty to ensure that students do not face any form of racial discrimination, including attacks and harassment.

### No easy answers

In a school day crammed with demands, dealing with bullying, especially racist bullying, is one of the most difficult problems facing teachers. There are no easy answers or instant solutions, but Kidscape has found the following suggestions to be effective.

Schools can ensure that:

- pupils are told from day one that bullying of any kind is not tolerated;
- they carry out an anonymous survey of the pupils to find out if racist bullying is a problem and then act upon it;
- parents are informed that the school is committed to ensuring racial harmony amongst its pupils, staff and the community;
- they have materials, books, lessons and activities which are used in the curriculum to help the pupils learn appropriate ways to behave;
- PSHE (Personal, Social and Health Education) modules cover prejudice, direct/indirect discrimination, stereotypes, celebrating diversity;
- their guidelines state that all pupils are entitled to feel safe and secure;
- their ethos is one which values and respects people from all cultural, ethnic and religious backgrounds;
- all staff and governors are trained in equality issues, working with parents, supporting victims, changing negative behaviour and school procedures for resolving bullying.

### Helping pupils

In order to support pupils, schools need to:

- work with staff and pupils together to create an anti-bullying policy that includes issues of racist bullying;
- ensure that the policy is readily available to staff, parents and pupils. Some schools ask pupils to sign the policy and keep it in their school file;
- explain that everyone has a part to play in preventing bullying – no one is allowed to be a bystander. Anyone who knows about or witnesses bullying, must tell and get help;
- act when told about racist or any kind of bullying;
- be aware and vigilant. If possible, the staff should try to uncover the bullying as this protects the victims from being seen as 'grassing' and further risking their safety;

- provide a private way for frightened victims to tell, such as individual meetings with all pupils on a regular basis so no one is seen to be singled out, or a box where children can anonymously post suggestions, complaints and comments;
- ensure that the PSHE programme includes lessons in self-esteem and friendship skills, assertiveness, handling conflict;
- teach all pupils bullying prevention programmes such as Kidscape which includes strategies such as:
    → ignore the bullying, pretend not to hear;
    → walk away quickly; use body language to look determined, strong and positive even if you feel frightened inside;
    → shout 'NO, GO AWAY' as loudly as possible;
    → always tell a trusted adult if you are bullied.

## Consequences

Pupils, parents and staff need to know that racist bullying will not be tolerated and what will happen if it persists.

It is important that schools:
- set up procedures for resolving incidents. A policy statement on its own is not enough – clear guidelines ensure action is taken;
- ensure the safety and support of victims;
- try first to mediate so that pupils are given a chance to resolve things peacefully, if possible;
- realise that some pupils do not appreciate the distress they are causing and are willing to change their behaviour;
- help bullies to understand that their behaviour is completely unacceptable and that they must take responsibility for their actions, apologise and make amends;

- use sanctions if initial attempts to stop the bullying fail;
- record repeated and or serious incidents of bullying so that trends in a class or with certain pupils can be monitored and stopped;
- inform parents/guardians about bullying incidents and what action is being taken – in serious cases, ask them to come to a meeting to discuss the problem;
- call the social services or police, if necessary and appropriate;
- make it clear that suspension or exclusion will be considered in serious cases.

- The above information is reprinted with kind permission from Kidscape, the charity committed to keeping children safe from abuse. For more information on bullying and other issues, please visit their website at www.kidscape.org.uk

© Kidscape

# Beat bullying

**If you are being bullied you might feel like there's no way out. Find out how to break that cycle right now and get rid of bullying for good**

### What is bullying?

Bullying usually involves a person or group exploiting the fact that they feel more powerful than another. This can be acted out through physical or emotional harm – or both. Bullying takes on many forms, such as: leaving people out of a social circle; racist and homophobic abuse; being singled out as 'different'; sexual abuse and discrimination; being taunted about your family situation; being forced to hand over money and possessions; and physical and violent attacks.

### Doesn't it just happen at school?

Bullying doesn't finish the minute you leave the school gates; it can happen to anyone at any age, and people can become bullies at any stage in life. Each week 500,000 young people are bullied in their community.

'Often bullying is described as a school thing but from our standpoint

it's a community issue,' says John Quinn at Beat Bullying. 'It affects people on buses, in the street, at work and at youth clubs. It can affect relationships between cousins and siblings and it can strike at any stage.'

### New ways of bullying

As technology develops and becomes more readily available, bullies are finding new and innovative ways to pick on their victims. 'Happy slapping' is the latest craze, where bullies take pictures or video clips of physical attacks to send on.

Texting and emailing threatening messages is another form of bullying that is on the rise, with one in five children now reporting that they have been bullied in this way.

### Beat bullying

- Body language: bullies pick on easy targets, so poor posture and averted eye contact will attract unwanted attention. Stand proud with your shoulders back and your head up, and look people in the eye – you'll soon give out the message that you're not afraid.
- Safety in numbers: this is particularly important when bullying is taking place outside of a regular establishment. Work out your safest and most public routes home and try to stick with others at all times.
- Walk away: if you find yourself in a situation that is making you feel uncomfortable, calmly but quickly walk away. If you are near other people or a public place, head in that direction.
- Speak up: this is exactly the thing that bullies expect you not to do, so you are already regaining some control by speaking up.

If the bullying is taking place in an established setting like a workplace or university, approach a colleague or tutor you are comfortable with – or try a student counsellor, an NUS rep, or the human resources department – all of whom have a duty to take these issues seriously and offer their help and support. It can be difficult to know who to turn to when bullying is happening outside the boundaries of regular establishments. Telling friends and family may help you feel more protected, but if they feel unable to solve the problem, contact the police.

■ Explore your feelings: if there is no one you can tell, or you just don't feel ready to open up face-to-face, consider talking anonymously to an organisation such as Bullying Online. You can send an email (help@bullying. co.uk) at any time of day, offering you the support you need without having to pluck up the courage to speak in person. You may find that keeping a diary of your thoughts and feelings also helps you to start facing the issue.

### Coping with childhood bullying as an adult

'Bullying is not a simple issue,' explains John Quinn. 'It can lead to stress, anxiety, depression and self-harm, all of which can follow young people into adult life.'

Adults can find it particularly hard trying to come to terms with the problems they faced as a child. Dragging up all those old memories is a painful process, and it can seem easier to keep repressing them than face them now, but pushing problems deeper down doesn't make them go away.

Start by opening up to a close friend or family member – or even by writing your feelings down on paper. You may find that simply sharing your bad memories in a kind and supportive environment is enough to help you move on. Other times, opening up to a friend can help people to realise just how much support they need. If this is the case, counselling may be the best route forward – you can talk to your GP about a referral or contact the British Association of Counselling and Psychotherapy. Alternatively, Quinn suggests talking to someone anonymously through a helpline such as Samaritans or Saneline.

■ The above information is re-printed with kind permission from TheSite.org. Visit www.thesite.org for more information.

© TheSite.org

# Don't blame the bullies!

**It's not their fault, say the schools that back support groups over punishment**

*By James Mills*

Teachers are being told not to punish bullies, it emerged yesterday.

Hundreds of schools are adopting a trendy approach which tells the thugs they are not at fault and encourages them to discuss their behaviour in 'support groups'.

Children's campaigners say the no-blame policy is putting pupils at risk, with some even attempting suicide because they feel nothing is being done to end their torment.

Despite this, they say, the strategy has been taken up in areas such as Bristol, Birmingham, Worcestershire, Kent and Hertfordshire.

Growing support for the approach suggests that the Government's anti-bullying measures, announced this week, could be largely ignored by many heads because it is left to individual schools to develop their own policies.

The issue erupted in the Commons yesterday when Labour MP Dan Morris claimed Bristol City Council was 'calling on its teachers not to punish or blame pupils who bully other pupils.'

He called the policy 'dangerous and reckless', and added: 'It does nothing for the victims and does nothing to make bullies change their behaviour.'

Despite the apparent widespread use of the 'no-blame' technique, Tony Blair said he was 'shocked' to hear about it.

The Prime Minister added: 'I profoundly disagree with the decision that council has taken. Bullying should be punished.'

Schools Minister Jacqui Smith this week promised powers to help schools tackle thuggery, including court orders which could fine parents of persistent bullies up to £1,000.

But the children's charity Kidscape warned that the 'no blame' approach was gaining support across the country.

It was developed by former teacher George Robinson and educational psychologist Barbara Maines in 1992. They launched a company, Lucky Duck Publishing, to promote it.

Teachers are told to act in the belief that bullies want to stop behaving as they do. They are brought together in groups to discuss their behaviour. Their victims are interviewed and told to write about their feelings of unhappiness. This is then shown to the bullies.

The theory assumes that the bullies will be moved by the distress of their victim.

Kidscape director Michele Elliott described it as a 'charter for bullies'. She said she had received 'countless' complaints from parents whose bullied children were continuing to suffer.

Many have taken their children out of schools which refuse to punish bullies. Some children have even attempted suicide.

Miss Elliott said: 'We are very concerned about this. Hundreds of schools are using it. We have a file full of letters from parents whose children continue to suffer because schools are failing them in this way.

'In many cases the bullies actually use the information they learn about the victim in these sessions against them.

'Children need to learn that there are consequences to their actions. This trendy, flawed "no blame" approach only reinforces the idea that actions, including bullying, have no consequences.

'It is a charter for bullies and a recipe for disaster for victims.'

Jos Clark, of Bristol Council's children's services committee, admitted its guidelines included the 'no blame' approach. But she said it was one of several options open to schools.

'Bullying is a complex matter,' she added. 'In the guidelines we do not advocate or promote any single method.'

Mr Robinson, 60, defended his technique. He said: 'It keeps the victims safe and is more likely to change the behaviour of bullies than punishing them.

'Most bullying is teasing and this method works. That's why so many schools are taking it up.'

Last week, the Government's newly appointed 'children's tsar' claimed that virtually every pupil in the country is affected in some way by bullying.

Children's Commissioner Al Aynsley-Green blamed an increasingly violent society.

A spokesman for the Department for Education and Skills said: 'Bullying should be punished. So-called "no blame" approaches should not allow bullies to escape without punishment.'

■ This article first appeared in the *Daily Mail*, 24 November 2005.

# Bullying in schools

## Schools must do more to tackle bullying, say children and young people

**5**2 per cent of children and young people say that bullying is a big problem in their school, according to a new survey for the Anti-Bullying Alliance – and the same number think that schools are not doing enough to tackle the issue.

More than 500 seven to 19-year-olds across the UK were consulted for the survey, which was carried out by the British Market Research Bureau (BMRB) ahead of national Anti-Bullying Week next week (21-25 November).

The findings suggest that older children are more likely to feel that schools could do more to tackle bullying. Only 27 per cent of 15 to 19-year-olds thought that schools were doing enough, against 67 per cent of seven to 10-year-olds.

Younger children were also more likely to feel that schools were doing well in involving students in tackling bullying. 65 per cent of seven to 10-year-olds thought this was the case, whereas only 33 per cent of 15 to 19-year-olds agreed.

'We know that many schools are doing their best to address the scourge of bullying, but as recent incidents of violence show, this is still not good enough,' commented Vanessa Cooper, coordinator of the Anti-Bullying Alliance. 'Today's findings indicate that more needs to be done, especially to support and protect older children.

'Our message is clear. Bullying is unacceptable, and all schools must take action to tackle it.'

The survey follows comments from the Children's Commissioner for England, Al Aynsley Green, who is treating bullying as one of his key priorities. The commissioner has been working closely with the Anti-Bullying Alliance and will be delivering the keynote speech at an Alliance conference in London on Monday 21 November to launch Anti-Bullying Week.

The Alliance has also produced a special pack for schools, with 50 suggestions for Anti-Bullying Week activities. The pack includes a questionnaire that schools can use to monitor levels of bullying and a checklist for action in the longer term.

*14 November 2005*

■ The above information is reprinted with kind permission from the Anti-Bullying Alliance. For more information, please visit the Anti-Bullying Alliance website at www.anti-bullyingalliance.org

### Where homophobic bullying occurs in schools

| Type of bullying | Corridors | Classrooms | School grounds | Changing rooms | On the way home | Other places |
|---|---|---|---|---|---|---|
| Called names | XXX | XXX | | X | | X |
| Teased | | | | X | | |
| Hit/kicked | | | XX | | XX | |
| Frightened by look/stare | X | XX | | XX | XX | X |
| Rumour-mongering | XX | | | X | | |
| Public ridicule | XX | XXX | XX | X | X | |
| Sexual assault | | | | X | | |
| Belongings taken | | | X | X | | |

x = sometimes; xx = regularly; xxx = frequently

Source: *Rivers 2000. Taken from the Department of Health report 'Stand Up For Us' (Crown copyright).*

# Understanding the bully

**What could be worse than being called in to your child's school and told that he or she is a bully? You may feel like punishing them, but kids who bully often have underlying insecurities. By Hilary Pereira**

The many charities and helplines set up to tackle bullying offer a lot of advice and support to the victims, but there are fewer resources available for parents of children who bully. It's vital for parents to recognise their child's behaviour and learn to understand what could be motivating him or her to pick on their peers.

> *'Many children don't know themselves why they bully. Not only do they not fully understand – some don't have a clue they are bullies'*

'Many children don't know themselves why they bully,' says Peter Sharp, a chartered psychologist who focuses on special educational needs and emotional literacy. 'Not only do they not fully understand – some don't have a clue they are bullies,' he explains.

### What is bullying?

The child, or group of children, that bullies is wielding power over their target. Bullying behaviour includes the following:

- verbal abuse;
- humiliating, taunting and be-littling another child;
- alienating, isolating and exclud-ing another child;
- blackmail and threatening be-haviour;
- making another child do things he or she doesn't want to do;
- physical attacks;
- damaging another child's belong-ings;
- stealing or demanding money from the target child;

- spreading malicious rumours;
- attacking when the other child is most vulnerable.

### Why do children bully?

We all need self-esteem, and children are no different. Children who are feeling bad about themselves or going through a difficult time may try to become more confident through exercising power over others. 'Research shows that many children who bully have themselves been bullied – either by children or adults,' Peter Sharp comments.

Other reasons why kids bully include being jealous of the target child or feeling insecure because they are in some way different from their peers. In this last case, a bully might decide to pose as a tough-guy, as a defence mechanism against other children's potential teasing.

Some kids are simply carrying on behaviour they have learnt at home:

if rows between siblings or parents are frequently 'resolved' with verbal abuse or even flying fists, a child will learn that indulging in this bullyish behaviour is the way to come out on top. Many children who bully do not understand how wrong their actions are, or how desperate it makes their victims feel.

### Ways you can help your child

Instead of dishing out punishment after punishment, it's far more helpful to try to understand what is motivating your child to bully others. Ask yourself whether any of the following may be having an adverse influence of his or her behaviour:

- the arrival of a new baby or other major life change;
- integration into a new stepfamily;
- constant criticism or punishment at home;
- being bullied by a third party;
- feelings of inadequacy or low self-esteem.

Talk to your child about his or her reasons for bullying – it may be helpful to involve a third party, such as a trusted adult friend or relative.

'Get your child to imagine how he would feel if he lost his favourite toy,' suggests Peter Sharp, 'and talk about how it feels to be rejected by a friend or excluded from a group. Then discuss how those feelings may be similar to how the child being bullied feels, and work out together how to make amends.'

Try these techniques to help your child change:

- talk about the reasons for the bullying and explain how it makes the victim feel;
- discourage similar behaviour amongst family members;

---

*Many children who bully do not understand how wrong their actions are, or how desperate it makes their victims feel*

---

- discuss the problem with your child's teacher;
- show your child how to join in with other children without bullying;
- role play, in which the bully takes the role of victim to see how it feels to be on the receiving end;
- uncover feelings of low self-esteem and try to address them;
- give plenty of praise and encouragement when your child shows kindness to others.

If you find it difficult to get through to your child, you may need help from an outside counsellor or therapist (ask your GP for a referral).

Every school is obliged to have an anti-bullying policy, so the head-teacher and class teachers should all be able to offer appropriate help.

## How bullies can help others

Sometimes children who have been bullies are the best people to help reform other bullies. Through counselling, it's possible to turn the situation round and help bullies see the devastating effect they can have on their victims and victims' families. Placing them in the supervised position of coach and mentor can build their self-esteem in a way that bullying other children never could,

and it can also give them a chance to make amends for their previous behaviour.

### Recommended reading

- *Nurturing Emotional Literacy: A Practical Guide* by Peter Sharp (David Fulton Publishers, £17 from www.amazon.co.uk).
- *Your Child Bullying* by Jenny Alexander (Vega Books, £5.99 from www.amazon.co.uk).
- *The Bullying Problem: How to deal with difficult children* by A. T. Train (Souvenir Press, £9.99 from www. amazon.co.uk).

- Information from iVillage UK. Visit www.iVillage.co.uk for more information.

© *iVillage UK*

# Rise of the brat-bully

**Spoiled and spiteful, pupils whose parents believe they are angels**

A new breed of middle-class bullies regarded as 'little gods' at home are making their classmates' lives a misery, it was claimed yesterday.

'Little Miss Sunshine' or 'Little Mr Wonderful' do not fit the prototype of the thugs most associated with picking on other children.

But indulged at home and influential at school, they have the power to wreak havoc in the classroom, according to Michele Elliott, director of children's charity Kidscape.

The parents of such bullies find it almost impossible to believe their 'perfect child' is capable of bad behaviour.

---

*By Sarah Harris, Education Correspondent*

---

But thanks to their over-indulgent parenting, the children go to school believing they are 'little gods' who should be adored by all.

The warning comes as a head-teachers' leader has already revealed millions of middle-class children are under-performing at school because their parents are too soft to enforce a proper routine at home.

Miss Elliott told the Commons' Education Select Committee yester-

day: 'In addition to children coming from homes where bullying is basically fostered, we found a whole other group of bullies who come from homes where they are so indulged that they go to school and they are little gods.

'They think that everything revolves around them. We call them the "brat bullies".'

Speaking after the hearing, she claimed these children tended to come from nice homes where they were 'given absolutely everything emotionally and materialistically'. Their parents often sat on school governing bodies.

Her charity's helpline receives 16,000 calls a year, many from parents and children worried about bullies.

She said many parents had pointed out that the 'kid bullying my kid isn't a horrible thug who goes out mugging people – it's Little Miss Sunshine or Little Mr Wonderful'.

Miss Elliott said: 'They rule the roost. They go into school and feel they are entitled to the same sort of adoration that they get at home.

'They expect the teachers and all the other kids to kow-tow to them.

'If they don't, they start to bully the other children. They are supported by their parents and feel that the world owes them.

'I have some sympathy for these parents because they think they have raised this perfect child.

'They can't believe this child is going and inflicting misery on other kids. That can be a very powerful child.'

The Committee heard girls in particular used 'rumour-mongering' and 'social isolation' to control their victims.

David Moore, a senior Ofsted inspector, highlighted the use of 'non-verbal communication' as a powerful playground weapon.

---

### 'They think that everything revolves around them. We call them the "brat bullies"'

---

He cited the example of a group of girls who walk up to another girl who thinks they are all friends. They then walk away, cutting her dead and leaving her publicly humiliated.

'Nothing is said but that actually diminishes the youngster in self-esteem and self-confidence,' he said.

A recent study from educational psychologist Valerie Besag found girls were more effective bullies than boys and used psychological warfare to dominate their victims.

Miss Elliott said 'brat bullies' would not harass anyone physically because that would be proof of their bad behaviour.

She said: 'It is mental bullying, usually of those children who don't bow down to them – such things as "sending someone to Coventry", starting rumours about them, pretending to be friends and then letting them down publicly.

'The princess behaviour we hear about involves arranging parties and excluding one person or encouraging someone to hold a party and then persuading everyone else not to go.'

■ This article first appeared in the *Daily Mail*, 11 May 2006.

# Are you bullying someone?

## Information from ChildLine

**B**ullies don't just come from out of the blue. Often bullies have had a bad experience themselves or they feel insecure or unhappy with their life. It doesn't make what they do right but understanding what might lie behind their behaviour can sometimes help the situation.

What if you're the one doing the bullying? You know that what you're doing and saying is hurting people but you just can't stop yourself. What can you do?

### Jay's story

'There's this boy in our class, Carl. He was a right pain, I mean, he just whinged about everything. I once told him he was a wimp and he cried and the awful thing was that I felt good seeing him cry. The others laughed and that made me feel even better. Then it got to be a habit. People copied me and I got even worse and said really horrible things. Then I started hiding his stuff and I really enjoyed seeing him panic and

run about getting hysterical. I used to think it was funny.'

Jay didn't think much about his behaviour until one day when his class teacher said that Carl was in hospital because he'd tried to hurt himself to get away from the bullying.

'It had only been a bit of fun really – I hadn't realised how it made him feel. I didn't mean him to take it seriously. I rang ChildLine and said

I was afraid that there was something wrong with me. I mean it's not normal to like hurting people is it? The counsellor was great. He talked to me about my family, how Dad had treated me just like I'd treated Carl when I cried, and how I felt when he did it. I even sort of understood my dad a bit better. The counsellor asked me if I had anyone I could talk to about it all. In the end I talked to my uncle. He's Mum's brother and we go to football together. He helped me get back into the habit of helping people out rather than putting them down and made me feel better about myself. I even apologised to Carl for what I'd done. It was difficult but I'm glad I did and now I don't feel like there's something wrong with me.'

■ The above information is re-printed with kind permission from ChildLine. Visit www.childline.org.uk for more information. ChildLine and the NSPCC joining together for children.

# Important facts and figures

## Information from Beat Bullying

- Each week at least 450,000 young children are bullied at school.
- Each week a further 500,000 are bullied outside of school in the community.
- Every year 40,000 young people telephone helplines about bullying.
- More than one in five severely-bullied children will attempt to take their own life.
- Bullying worsens social exclusion.
- Victims of bullying lack confidence, often have few friends, spend their leisure time alone, and often suffer from anxiety, sleep problems, depression and even suicide (Royal College of Psychiatrists).
- One in every two school exclusions and 46% of school non-attendance is in some way related to bullying (Institute of Education).
- Bullying has a damaging effect on educational attainment.
- Under Article 28 of the United Nations Convention on the Rights of the Child (ratified by the UK in December 1991), schools should have a bullying policy and each child should be informed of what to do if they find themselves being bullied.
- Headteachers must have a policy to prevent bullying among pupils and will need to satisfy themselves that it complies with the Human Rights Act 1998.
- Under the School Standards and Framework Act 1998, s.61(4)b, schools have certain statutory responsibilities regarding behaviour: 'the head teacher shall determine measures (which may include the making of rules and provisions for enforcing them) to be taken with a view to … b) encouraging good behaviour and respect for others on the part of pupils and, in particular, preventing all forms of bullying among pupils.'
- Section 175 of the Education Act 2002 sets out the requirements

for governing bodies in relation to the welfare of children in their school: 'The governing body of a maintained school shall make arrangements for ensuring that their functions relating to the conduct of the school are exercised with a view to safeguarding and promoting the welfare of children who are pupils at the school.'

- The Education Act 2002 sets out two broad aims for the National Curriculum and schools should ensure that it: (i) 'provides opportunities for all pupils to learn and achieve'; (ii) 'promotes the spiritual, moral, cultural, mental and physical development of pupils at the school and of society, and prepares pupils at the school for the opportunities, responsibilities and experiences of later life'.

- The DfES circular, *Social Inclusion: Pupil Support Circular 10/99*, outlines government expectations and the legal duty of headteachers with regard to bullying. It specifically mentions bullying behaviour related to race, sexual orientation, a child's appearance, behaviour or special educational needs.
- The National Health School Guidance states that schools should have 'a policy and code of practice for tackling bullying, which is owned, understood and implemented by all members of the school community and includes contact with external support agencies'.
- Under the Race Relations (Amendment) Act 2000, schools are required to promote race equality rather than to simply react to racist incidents, and good practice indicates that the requirements of the Act should be linked to a school's anti-bullying policy.

- The above information is reprinted with kind permission from Beat Bullying. Visit www.beatbullying.org for more information.

© Beat Bullying

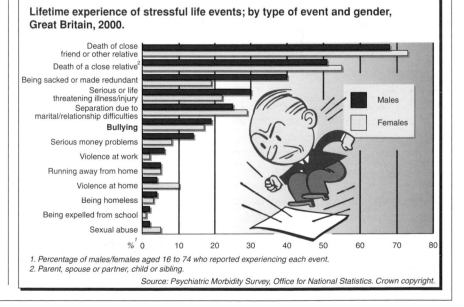

### Stressful life events

Lifetime experience of stressful life events; by type of event and gender, Great Britain, 2000.

1. Percentage of males/females aged 16 to 74 who reported experiencing each event.
2. Parent, spouse or partner, child or sibling.

Source: Psychiatric Morbidity Survey, Office for National Statistics. Crown copyright.

# Back to bullying?

## Does back to school mean back to bullying?

As the summer holidays draw to a close, counsellors at leading children's charity ChildLine are providing comfort and advice to thousands of desperate children scared to return to school for fear of the bullies who may be waiting for them. The charity is urging schools to be on the alert for children who need help – and to nip bullying in the bud right at the start of the new term.

ChildLine is especially concerned that many children who are fearful of returning to school didn't even get a break from the bullies during the holidays. Figures released by the charity today (31 August) reveal that just under 5,000 children were counselled about bullying during the summer holidays last year – and the situation looks likely to be the same this summer.

The charity's counsellors are taking calls from children as young as nine who say they have been called names or attacked when they were out and about, or have been sent abusive or threatening text messages during the holidays.

Lindsay Gilbert, Head of Child-Line In Partnership With Schools, says: 'Sometimes it can be easy for schools to think that the bullying has gone away over the summer break, and when a new school year begins children may have new teachers who don't know there is a problem. Also, when children move to a new school they lose the support network of teachers and friends who may have helped them when they were being bullied.

'The start of a new school year is a busy time and it's easy for bullying to be overlooked, especially if children are in a new, unfamiliar environment. It is vital that children know their school and parents are still aware of the problem, are ready to listen, and will take action quickly to make sure the bullying stops.'

ChildLine has a wealth of advice on offer to schools that want to tackle bullying. The charity pioneered the highly successful technique of peer support, where pupils receive training to act as first points of contact for any child at the school who needs help. Young people tell ChildLine they often find it easier to talk to another pupil rather than a teacher, and peer support has been proven to reduce bullying and make the whole school a better place to be.

Lindsay Gilbert says: 'For most children a new school year will be an exciting and happy time but if you are feeling daunted, worried or fearful please don't keep your problems bottled up. Talk to a friend, a parent, or a teacher, or if you need to talk anonymously please call ChildLine on 0800 1111.'

For more information about ChildLine's innovative work with schools and tips on tackling bullying log on to www.childline.org.uk. *31 August 2005*

■ The above information is reprinted with kind permission from ChildLine. Visit www.childline.org. uk for more information. ChildLine and the NSPCC joining together for children.

© NSPCC

---

## Calls to ChildLine

***Children calling ChildLine about bullying during the school holidays***
*(All identifying details have been changed)*

Gemma, ten, called ChildLine and said that she had been bullied by some girls from her school. She said, 'I was in the park with my friend and these girls came and started calling us 'fat cows' and 'fleabags'. They used to be our friends.' Gemma told her counsellor that she didn't want to tell her parents about the bullying. 'I don't want to upset them,' she said.

Fiona, 11, told her ChildLine counsellor, 'I start secondary school next week, it's a big school and I've heard from friends that there is bullying there.' Fiona said she was scared because none of her friends from primary school would be moving with her.

David, 15, said, 'I'm starting a new school but I'm worried about how I'll cope.' David told ChildLine that he was dyslexic and thought that his new teachers wouldn't give him the support he had experienced at his last school. He said: 'I got one-to-one support at my last school. I'm really anxious about the demands for work to be done on time. And at the last school I was bullied – it got sorted out but now I'll be with different teachers.'

Neesha, 12, called ChildLine and said: 'I was out shopping with some friends yesterday and some boys from school saw us and started calling us 'bitches' and 'slags'. We shouted back at them but then they came over and threatened to beat us up when they saw us next term.' Neesha told her counsellor that she had talked to her parents but they had just advised them to stay away from the boys. Neesha said, 'It's hard because one of my friends lives near one of the boys so she sees him all the time.'

Sam, nine, called because he was worried about being bullied when he went back to school in September. He said, 'I got bullied last term and I told a teacher but they didn't do anything. I fight back sometimes and get into trouble. It's not fair.' Sam told ChildLine that one of his teachers had said that the bullying would prepare him for secondary school. 'I don't even like hanging round with my friends anymore in case they get into trouble,' he said.

# Helping friends beat bullying

**Speaking up can be the hardest thing to do if you're being bullied, so if you're worried about a friend, make it as easy as possible for them to tell you. Here's our advice**

### Picking up on the signs

Many people will go to extraordinary lengths to hide the fact that they are being bullied, so it can be difficult to detect. However, there are some signs you can look out for:

- physical injuries such as cuts or bruises that cannot be explained;
- ripped or damaged clothes;

*If you are worried about a friend, the best approach is to gently let them know that you are concerned about their wellbeing*

- regular complaints of illness (such as feeling sick or headaches) can be a cover up for simply wanting to avoid certain situations;
- mood swings;
- anxiety/nervousness;
- acting depressed, upset or tearful;
- low self-esteem and loss of confidence;
- acting rude, hostile or defensive;
- withdrawing from group interaction, physical contact and avoiding eye contact;
- a change in eating habits;
- alcohol and drug use;
- self-harming;
- frequently losing money and other items;
- tired and lacking energy.

Be aware, however, that many of the indicators above are also signs of other emotional problems and do

**TheSite.org**

not immediately mean that bullying is the cause.

### The gently, gently approach

If you are worried about a friend, the best approach is to gently let them know that you are concerned about their wellbeing. Be sensitive and pick a time when you won't be interrupted. Listen to what they say and support their wishes. If they are being bullied, remind them that help is available and that having told you is the first step towards getting help.

### Face bullies together

- Identify when and where the bullying is happening and make sure you – or someone else – is accompanying them at these times.
- Stick up for your friend if you see them being bullied.
- Encourage them to report the bullying to someone else. If it is in an established setting, such as university or work, you could go with them to get advice from a student counsellor, NUS or someone in the human resources department. If the bullying is taking part in the community, they can report it to the police.
- Dealing with bullies is one thing, dealing with emotions is another. Keep offering your support, even after the bullying stops – and if they are finding it hard to move forwards, encourage them to seek emotional support from an organisation such as Saneline or Samaritans.

- The above information is reprinted with kind permission from TheSite.org. Visit www.thesite.org for more information.

© TheSite.org

# Two out of three teenage girls admit to bullying

**Schools are failing to stem growing tide of abuse between children, survey shows**

A vicious cycle of bullying by teenage girls has been uncovered. A survey reveals that while two out of three girls admit abusing others, more than 90 per cent say they have been bullied themselves.

Few bullies in the survey admitted to worrying about their behaviour, with one-third saying they 'felt fine' after bullying someone because 'they deserved it'.

The survey, by the NSPCC and *Sugar* magazine, of almost 1,000 young girls across the country found that more than one in four teenagers have been abused by children they consider to be their friends.

> *Over one in five of the teenage girls who responded to the survey said they had bullied someone because they didn't like them*

Sadie Sale, a 19-year-old former victim of bullying who turned into a bully, said: 'It is so easy to become a bully, especially if you've been bullied yourself. I was so desperate to be left alone that I would have done anything, including making someone else's life a misery, just to make it stop. I hate what I did and am working hard to make up for it.'

Over one in five of the teenage girls who responded to the survey said they had bullied someone because they didn't like them. One in 20 said they were simply 'doing it for a laugh'.

Chris Cloke, Head of Child Protection at the NSPCC, said: 'The results of this survey are a sad reflection of the culture of bullying.

It's shocking to see that even though the majority have experienced the pain of being bullied this has not stopped them from bullying others.

'Many schools are trying to tackle bullying effectively but we need to ensure that anti-bullying policies not only support the victims but also change the behaviour of the bullies,' he added. According to the survey, conducted as part of a 'Stand Up, Speak Out' campaign by the magazine and the charity, schools are failing to tackle the problem.

One 16-year-old girl, who asked to remain anonymous, said, 'I was bullied at start of year 10 by the people I thought were my friends. The school didn't do anything and so I was off school for 18 months because I was too scared to go in.

'The school kept denying that they had any problem with bullying and ended up taking me to court because I was too scared to go in.'

More than 70 per cent of the respondents said they felt that bullying in school was still a problem or had got worse. Only 2 per cent said they would tell a teacher if they were being bullied.

'Children are scared and embarrassed to tell teachers what is happening to them,' said Annabel Brog, the editor of *Sugar*.

'If they get caught snitching or the teacher deals with their complaint badly, the bullying can escalate.'

Bullies used all methods at their disposal to abuse their victim, the research found, with nearly half admitting they had used verbal abuse; 13 per cent said they had physically hurt another person. A similar number had sent deliberately intimidating text messages.

More than a quarter of the victims claimed to have felt suicidal as a result of being bullied; among them was Sarah who had been bullied since she was in primary school.

'It always used to be by people who I didn't like anyway but last year, I was bullied by my so-called friends,' she said. 'Suddenly, out of nowhere, they started saying horrible things about me. It was so awful, I wanted to kill myself.'

Sarah eventually told the teachers about being bullied but, she said, that made the situation worse: 'My old friends started picking on me even more. Soon these girls from the year below kept coming to find me and asking to have a fight. I am now really scared for my own safety.'

The survey results came as two children's support charities – Kidscape and the Yorkshire-based Bullying Online – denounced the organisation behind the government's Anti-Bullying Week as a waste of public funds.

The criticism came in response to details, provided to *The Observer*, of how the Anti-Bullying Alliance spent its £600,000 in government funding. Both charities said the money would have been better used dealing directly with victims of bullying.

*20 November 2005*

© *Guardian Newspapers Limited 2006*

# Girls and bullying

**Parents reveal the real picture**

Schoolgirl bullies are using increasingly sophisticated ways of bullying, according to a new report by Parentline Plus.

Research carried out by the parenting charity found that bullying by girls is becoming more underhand with a devastating effect on the victims – increasing the risks of suicide and self-harm.

Now, in the week of International Women's Day (March 8), the charity is calling on schools to be more proactive in making children and young people aware that bullying is not just a physical activity and those anti-bullying policies must reflect the different methods used by boys and girls.

Rumour-spreading, writing graffiti about their victims, alienating them from their classmates and the use of email and instant messaging are all ways of bullying used by girls, as well as hair-pulling, pushing and fighting.

'Because girls and bullying are difficult to identify, the invisibility of girls' difficulties has serious consequences in terms of their ability to access help,' said Dorit Braun, Chief Executive of Parentline Plus.

'Girls tend to internalise their feelings and to suffer from low self-esteem, depression and anxiety and it is important that those working with schoolchildren look out for these warning signs.'

In response to these concerns, Parentline Plus has produced a range of information materials, developed a special section on its website and continues to offer a listening ear to parents needing to talk about bullying.

In one particularly distressing call to the helpline, a parent said: 'My daughter left a distressing note on our bed one night telling us that she was being bullied at school. We approached her the next morning to find out what has been happening. She told us that a few girls had deliberately excluded her

## Parentline plus

in playground gatherings and would taunt her and make fun of her. A survey has been done in her class by one of the girls to find out 'who hated her'. Then they gave her the finished survey, which devastated her.'

Parentline Plus carried out its research during a three-month period. The research included an in-depth look at calls to the helpline about bullying, a survey of parents on its website and consultation with focus groups involving four groups of parents from different parts of the country.

Findings include:
- nearly 700 calls to the helpline about physical bullying;
- nearly 1,000 calls about verbal bullying;
- girls who are bullied may be at increased risk of bottling up their feelings, in the form of depression, anxiety, self-harm or withdrawal;

- withdrawn children may be increasingly likely to be victims of bullying, and bullying may cause withdrawn behaviour;
- all parents tried to talk to their children and then generally went to the school for help. However, several felt frustrated by lack of action and understanding within the school
- parents want greater resources given to the issue of bullying, greater discipline in schools and more publicity about what constitutes bullying today.

'Bullying is hugely complex and a very distressing issue,' added Dorit. 'The stories parents have told us demonstrate how malicious bullying by girls can be.'

During the Parentline Plus consultations, parents identified the following specific behaviours used by girls when they were bullying:
- taunting, name-calling, rumour-spreading;
- graffiti in toilets and other areas;
- blanking 'skanking', exclusion, alienation of friends;
- use of SMS, email, instant messaging, defamatory websites, phone calls;
- taking possessions;
- extortion (money);

- threats/intimidation;
- hair pulling, pushing;
- fighting or other physical aggression.

Another caller told the helpline: 'She kept her feelings to herself about the bullying, verbal and physical. She became suicidal, felt sick every day, didn't want to go. We think it's because she is shy, quiet, pretty and an easy target. We had meetings with school, police, the educational welfare officer and school counsellor. We eventually took her out of school because nothing was getting better, and she didn't feel safe. She was home-tutored for a while and then went to a special unit for children with medical needs.'

---

*While much more needs to be done to stop bullying, it is encouraging that the research shows schools can make a difference once they acknowledge that bullying does happen*

---

**Parentline Plus tips if your child says that they are being bullied**

- Listen and talk to them. They may feel out of control and ashamed – whether they are being bullied or bullying. Let them know you love them and want to help.
- Be clear that it is important for the bullying to stop and that the school will need to be involved.
- If your child is bullying others, think about what might be behind it – are they trying to get attention or fit in with the crowd, or are they unaware of how they are hurting others?
- Talk to the school as soon as possible.
- If you think things are not getting any better, ask to see the school's anti-bullying policy and make an appointment to see the headteacher.

Parentline Plus is also calling for schools to build good home-school communications, even where there

are no bullying problems, so that parents are able to trust the school and communicate openly about their worries with headteachers, teachers and other professionals.

The Parentline Plus research is being supported by the Advisory Centre for Education (ACE). Spokeswoman Liz Williams said: 'ACE welcomes Parentline Plus's latest research on girls and bullying and the experiences of parents. The research bears out what parents say to us on our advice lines about the bullying their children face in school. While much more needs to be done to stop bullying, it is encouraging that the research shows schools can make a difference once they acknowledge that bullying does happen on their premises, and when they work with parents to help both the bullied and the bullies.'
8 March 2006

- The above information is reprinted with kind permission from Parentline Plus. Visit www.parentlineplus.org.uk for more information.

© *Parentline Plus*

# Victims of bullying rarely ask for help

## Information from the British Psychological Society

P ast research has shown us just how damaging bullying can be, but what prevents victims of bullying asking for help?

Nathalie Noret and colleagues from the Social Inclusion Diversity Research Unit at York St John's College have investigated help-seeking behaviours among adolescent victims of bullying, to examine if the type of bullying and severity of bullying plays a role in the victim's seeking help.

Nathalie Noret will present her research on Friday 1 April 2005, at the British Psychological Society's Annual Conference at the University of Manchester.

A total of 1,860 pupils aged between 13 and 19 years old took part in the research by completing confidential questionnaires. 28.4% of the pupils reported being bullied. Only a small proportion of these victims reported talking to a teacher or someone at home about the bullying and it was pupils who were more severely bullied who were more likely to seek help from teachers or someone at home.

Nathalie Noret said: 'Help-seeking behaviour can be an effective coping strategy for victims of bullying. Encouraging victims to confide in parents or teachers about bullying plays a fundamental role in intervention strategies.

'Understanding the reasons why victims may not seek help can help teachers and researchers to build on existing intervention strategies and provide better support for victims of bullying.'
2 April 2005

- The above information is reprinted with kind permission from the British Psychological Society. Visit www.bps.org.uk for more information.

© *British Psychological Society*

# Bullying 'affects almost every child in Britain'

By Matthew Hickley, Home Affairs Correspondent

Virtually every pupil in the country is affected by an epidemic of bullying in schools, the Government's 'children's tsar' claimed yesterday.

Labour's newly-appointed Children's Commissioner Al Aynsley-Green blamed an increasingly violent society for what he said was now an almost universal problem.

He called on ministers to force schools to give every pupil a questionnaire on bullying each term.

But last night campaigners cast doubt on his claims, and said more bureaucracy was the last thing schools needed to help stamp out bullying.

They warned that valuable initiatives risked snowballing into a 'self-serving industry' which would divert scarce resources away from schools.

Professor Aynsley-Green was appointed by the Government in March as England's first Children's Commissioner, a £100,000-a-year post which involves 'promoting awareness of the views and interests of children' and examining key issues.

Yesterday, he chose bullying as the subject of his first high-profile initiative, claiming there was still 'a lot of denial' about the extent of the problem.

He told *The Observer*: 'I have had hundreds of in-depth conversations with children since accepting this post and I can tell you that one thing every child I have met has been affected by, with virtually no exceptions, is bullying.'

He added: 'I have no doubt that children are being brought up in a society where violence is the norm in many ways. I include in this the violence on television, in the workplace and in the home.'

Yesterday, Professor Aynsley-Green called for compulsory questionnaires for all school pupils to help uncover the true scale of bullying.

According to the ChildLine charity, the number of bullied children contacting its helpline has increased sharply in recent years.

But some doubt whether bullying has recently reached historically high levels, suggesting that greater awareness is bringing an age-old problem into the open. Chris Cloke, Head of Child Protection Awareness at the NSPCC, said: 'There is a need for more research in this area.

'I don't think we know if bullying is getting worse.

'Greater awareness means there is more reporting of cases, which is to be welcomed, and the complexity of the problem is increasingly being recognised.

'I think schools need to develop their own different approaches.'

Hugh McKinney, of the National Family Campaign, said: 'Nobody disputes that bullying needs to be effectively stamped out but there is a great danger of this issue running out of control and becoming a self-serving industry in its own right, if we magnify the problem beyond the reality. We need more firmly-based evidence than a Government tsar simply announcing that every child he talks to has been bullied. That is not good enough.

'Schools are working hard to combat bullying and we should think carefully before burdening them with yet more layers of bureaucracy.'

Nick Seaton, of the Campaign for Real Education, said: 'The idea that you can solve a problem like bullying by having a new central commissioner throwing more money and bureaucracy at it is a dangerous one. Most initiatives like this that come from Whitehall don't end up working.

'There's no doubt bullying is a real problem but I am sure it is not universal, as is being suggested.

'I am uneasy at the idea of a "children's tsar" presenting the whole thing as a monstrous problem and wanting to tell schools what to do.'

Mr Seaton added: 'We should be putting more focus on the rights of schoolteachers and parents to maintain good order. They are the ones who have been working for years to combat bullying.'

Professor Al Aynsley-Green, a respected academic and clinician, is a former NHS adviser on children's health. He was interviewed by a panel of teenagers before being appointed to his current job.

■ This article first appeared in the *Daily Mail*, 14 November 2005.

# Anger management skills

**Academic calls for government to develop anger management skills training for bullies**

*Recent research from Brunel University recommends a form of children's community service for bullies and shows that:*

- *Bullies learn from external role models (i.e. soap opera characters) as well as parents.*
- *Girls are becoming increasingly violent.*

To mark Anti-Bullying Week, an expert on bullying from Brunel University is calling for the Government to develop a children's 'community rescue scheme' to teach bullies how to channel their anger into constructive activity. The move follows the academic's research into bullying, which shows that bullies learn their behaviour from their parents' inability to control anger, or, in the absence of adult male role models, from external sources such as characters in soap operas.

Dr Sally Henry, lecturer at Brunel University with a a PhD in bullying, comments that bullying is becoming more widespread and more complex, as technology opens up sinister new channels for aggression. Sally explains: 'My research shows that it's pretty much a case of 'like father, like son' – kids learn how to deal with difficult situations from adult role models like their parents. But in the absence of parental guidance, kids will look to other role models, for example, male characters in soap operas. With around 35 million people a week viewing soap operas like *EastEnders*, *Emmerdale*, *Coronation Street* and *Hollyoaks*, this is a real problem.

'Another worrying trend about today's bullying is not just the scale, but the sophistication and level of violence. Today's school bully can turn to both physical and psychological means, can threaten in person, via mobile phones or through the Internet. They bully in the playground, but also on the bus, or in the street. They may not even know their victim – as is the case with "happy slapping" – it's just an outlet for the bully to increase their standing with their fellow bullies. And whilst girl bullies have traditionally focused on the psychological side, with boys tending towards the physical, gender roles have now become blurred. Girls are increasingly violent – and boys use both forms of intimidation. This means schools have an increasingly tough job to detect bullying and deal with it.

'Whilst each school has a policy for dealing with bullying, it's really important to ensure firstly that this policy is put into practice, and secondly, that the schools don't simply suppress the bullies. Suppressed anger simply pops up elsewhere. It has to be released. That's why we need to develop a form of kids' community service – anger management rescue camps – involving bullies and other kids, as well as adults, in order to teach bullies how to deal with their anger. There should be no stigma attached to these camps: they would simply be an opportunity for children to learn how to deal with their emotions effectively, rather than take them out on others.'

Other recommendations from Dr Henry include:
- ensuring negative media images are not available to children;
- banning harmful food additives;
- providing free, quick support for families following family breakdown;
- offering benefits to employers who encourage flexible working for single mothers;
- promoting traditional values (talking, family meals, respecting the elderly);
- setting curfews for children who repeatedly offend;
- producing guidelines for best practice parenting (including ADHD and other disorders).

Dr Henry also offers schools recommendations to sit alongside existing anti-bullying policies:
- zero tolerance for bullies and those who reinforce bullying behaviour;
- local power to make quick decisions;
- immediate separation of bully and victim;
- offering places of safety for victims;
- ensuring parental accountability;
- video cameras to be placed in all areas of the school where bullying takes place (e.g. in school playgrounds, classrooms, corridors, canteens and by wash basins);
- peer support groups.

*22 November 2005*

- The above information is reprinted with kind permission from Brunel University. Visit www.brunel.ac.uk for more information.

© *Brunel University*

# What is online bullying?

## Information from BECTA

**W**ith increasing new communication technologies being made available to children and young people, there will always be a potential for them becoming a victim to online bullying.

An NCH survey, conducted in 2002, found that one in four children in the UK are bullied or threatened via their mobile phone or online. Recent figures from ChildLine (August 2004) report a significant rise in the number of children being counselled about bullying, with many saying that new technologies, such as text messaging and email, were a factor. This 21st century bullying technique, known as online bullying, e-bullying or cyberbullying, is defined as follows: 'the use of information and communication technologies such as email, [mobile] phone and text messages, instant messaging (IM), defamatory personal websites and defamatory personal polling websites, to support deliberate, repeated, and hostile behaviour by an individual or a group, that is intended to harm others.'
*Bill Belsey, www.cyberbullying.ca*

Children and young people are keen adopters of new technologies, but this can also leave them open to the threat of online bullying. An awareness of the issues and knowledge of methods for dealing with online bullying can help reduce the risks.

### Bullying by text message
Bullying by text message has become an unfortunate and unpleasant by-product of the convenience that SMS (short message service) offers. Texting is more casual than a phone call and messages can be sent and received at times when other communication is not convenient. It is also perceived as being more anonymous, particularly if the message is sent via a website. Sometimes text messages are sent to embarrass, threaten or bully someone. This can be particularly upsetting as the message can arrive when the receiver least expects it. Additionally, if the person's number is not listed in the receiver's address book then the receiver will not necessarily know who has sent the message.

Children should be advised to be careful about giving out their mobile phone number, and ask that those that have their number never pass it on. If only known and trusted friends know the number, the less likely it is to be abused in this way.

If being bullied by text message, children should immediately seek help from a teacher, parent or carer. They should not respond to the messages, but should keep a detailed diary recording information such as the content of the message, the date, the time, the caller ID or whether the number was withheld or not available. If space permits, the messages should also be stored on the phone in case they are needed later as evidence. Abuse in the form

of bullying should be reported to the mobile phone company who can take certain steps to try to resolve the situation, and in some instances it may also be necessary to involve the police.

In some cases it may be necessary, or easier, to change the mobile phone number or to purchase a new phone.

### Bullying by email
Like bullying by text message, email provides a reasonably 'anonymous' method of communication which bullies have seized upon to harass their victims.

If being bullied by email, children should not respond to the messages, but should seek help from a teacher, parent or carer. Likewise, if they receive an email message from an unknown sender, they should exercise caution over opening it, or ask an adult for assistance. Don't delete the message but keep it as evidence of bullying.

If the email is being sent from a personal email account, abuse should be reported to the sender's email service provider. Many email programs also provide facilities to block email from certain senders.

If the bullying emails continue, and the email address of the sender is not obvious, then it may be possible to track the address using special software. Your email service provider may be able to offer assistance in doing this.

In certain cases, it may be easier to change your email address, and exercise caution over who this new address is given to.

### Bullying within chat rooms or by instant messaging
Aside from the general risks of using chat rooms and IM services, these services are also used by bullies.

Chat is a way of communicating with numerous people at the same time by typing messages which immediately appear on screen in a virtual meeting place, known as a chat room. Chat rooms have an element of anonymity so children may often have the confidence to say things online which they would not say face to face. Whilst this can be a positive thing for some children, it can also lead to bullying. Groups are often formed in chat rooms, just as they would be in school, and can be used as a way of excluding or harassing others.

Children should be encouraged to always use moderated chat rooms, and to never give out personal information while chatting. If bullying does occur, they should not respond to messages, but should leave the chat room, and seek advice from a teacher, parent or carer. If using a moderated chat room, the system moderators should also be informed, giving as much detail as possible, so that they can take appropriate action.

IM is a form of online chat but is private between two, or more, people. The system works on the basis of 'buddy lists', where chat can only take place with those on your list. Children should only add people to their buddy list that they know, and reject requests from others to join their list. Although this effectively reduces the risk of being bullied by IM, abuse is still possible.

If a child is bullied or harassed by IM, the service provider should be informed giving the nickname or ID, date, time and details of the problem. The service provider will then take appropriate action which could involve a warning or disconnection from the IM service. If a child has experienced bullying in this way, it might also be worth re-registering for instant messaging with a new user ID.

### Bullying by websites

Although less common, bullying via websites is now becoming an issue. Such bullying generally takes the form of websites that mock, torment, harass or are otherwise offensive, often aimed at an individual or group of people.

If a child discovers a bullying website referring to them, they should immediately seek help from a teacher, parent or carer. Pages

---

*Like bullying by text message, email provides a reasonably 'anonymous' method of communication which bullies have seized upon to harass their victims*

---

should be copied and printed from the website concerned for evidence, and the Internet service provider (ISP) responsible for hosting the site should be contacted immediately.

The ISP can take steps to find out who posted the site, and request that it is removed. Many ISPs will outline their procedures for dealing with reported abuse in an acceptable use policy (AUP) which can be found on their website.

Additionally, many websites and forum services now provide facilities for visitors to create online votes and polls, which have been used by bullies to humiliate and embarrass their fellow pupils. Again, any misuse of such services should be reported to a teacher, parent or carer who should then take steps to contact the hosting website and request the removal of the poll.

■ The above information is reprinted with kind permission from BECTA. Visit www.becta.org.uk for more information.

© BECTA

# Playground bullies move into cyberspace

### Information from the British Psychological Society

**B**ullies are now using new technology – email and text messages – to bully children, even in their own homes. These are the results of a four-year study of bullying by Nathalie Noret of York St John's University College and Ian Rivers of Queen Margaret University College, Belfast.

The results of the research will be presented at the British Psychological Society's Annual Conference at the City Hall, Cardiff on Friday 31 March 2006.

The authors of the study surveyed 11,227 children for the last four years about their experiences of bullying. Nearly 15% said that they had received nasty or aggressive text messages or emails. And there is a steady year-on-year increase in the number of children who are being bullied using new technology.

According to Nathalie Noret, cyberbullying could be seen as 'a form of indirect bullying like gossip, that spreads quickly outside of the playground. Girls were more likely to report being bullied by email or SMS, something we see with other forms of indirect bullying.

'Acknowledging the high prevalence of this kind of bullying is important', says Noret, 'because most interventions in schools are based on the assumption that bullying is physical or occurs face-to-face. Teachers and parents need to realise that a child's mobile phone or computer isn't just a communication tool – it's also a way for a bully to reach children in their own homes.'
*31 March 2006*

■ The above information is reprinted with kind permission from the British Psychological Society. Visit www.bps.org.uk for more information.
© *British Psychological Society*

# Cyberbullying

## Information from Kidscape

### Text\video messaging

- Don't reply to text messaging (also known as SMS or EMS) or video messaging (also known as MMS) that is abusive or obscene. Your mobile service provider e.g. Orange, T-Mobile, Vodafone, etc. should have a number that you can ring to report abusive messaging. Try their websites for details.
- Be careful who you give phone numbers to and don't leave your mobile lying around when you are not there.

### Chatrooms or instant messaging (IM)

- Do not give out personal information.
- Give yourself an alias that doesn't give out anything about your age, gender or location.
- Don't respond to abusive posting – ignore them or log off. If you don't take time off and calm down you'll end up writing something you'll regret which will only make the situation worse.
- Think about what you write – it is very easy for people to get the wrong idea about what you write or how you write it.

### Email

- If you receive a nasty or abusive email (known as being flamed), don't reply. If it's from someone you think you know, like someone at school, they'll want some kind of reaction, just like they would if they were standing in front of you and bullying you. Don't give them the satisfaction of replying, and they'll probably stop.
- If they don't stop then you need to find out where the email is coming from. Using an email client like Outlook or Outlook Express, clicking the right mouse button over an email will reveal lots of details about where and who the email came from. You can then get your parents to contact the school or the service provider of the sender of the email.
- The email can also come from people that you don't know, (known as spamming) – email addresses are fairly easy for companies to obtain on the Internet, using software called email harvesters. They are also surprisingly easy for specialist computer programs to guess. Under no circumstances should you reply to these types of email, even if they have a 'Click here and stop receiving this email' link – this will just confirm your email address as a real one. The individual sending it can then sell or pass it on to other people and you'll be flooded with even more junk and abusive emails.
- You can delete the emails, but if the situation becomes serious, you should save them or print them off so that, if you do need to take action, you have some evidence.
- Learn more about your email program from the Help menu – you should be able to find details of how you can create folders, email filters and folder routeing. This won't stop the emails but it can help to shield you from them.

### Web

- If the cyberbullying is on a school or community website, do as you would do if the bullying was face-to-face – tell someone like your parents or teachers.
- If it's on a site that you don't know about, you have to do a bit of research to find out who hosts the website. There is a good article at Bullying Online about general online safety, with a section on how to get more details on possible owners of the website.

- The above information is re-printed with kind permission from Kidscape. Visit www.kidscape.org.uk for more information.

© Kidscape

# Putting 'U' in the picture

## Mobile bullying survey 2005

**B**ullying can ruin children's lives. The consequences of it can vary widely, from making children upset or unhappy to, in rare cases, suicide. Bullying via mobile phone is a new and particularly nasty form of bullying. This is why leading children's charity NCH has joined forces with Tesco Mobile to tackle this problem head-on. With 97 per cent of 12 to 16-year-olds owning a mobile phone, there is no time to lose.

### Why NCH and Tesco Mobile?

NCH was the first organisation to take up this issue at a national level and is the internationally recognised expert on mobile bullying. It commissioned the first-ever survey into mobile and online bullying in April 2002, pinpointing text bullying as a new and very modern problem. Tesco Mobile is a responsible mobile operator, at the forefront of initiatives to help tackle this issue, and is determined to help raise awareness of mobile bullying among young people and families.

### What do we mean by mobile bullying?

There are several ways someone can be bullied via a mobile phone. We define text bullying, the biggest mobile bullying problem, as one or more unwelcome text messages that the recipient finds threatening, or causes discomfort in some way. Very often bullies will disguise their numbers from the victim and in some cases they use other people's phones to avoid being caught.

Camera phones may be used to make the victim feel threatened, embarrassed or uncomfortable. Photographs could be sent to other people. Someone may receive silent calls, abusive messages or their identity may even be stolen and used to harass others who then think the victim is responsible. Bullying or threatening messages have been sent through websites using the names and phone numbers of people who knew nothing about it.

### Why is mobile bullying such an important issue?

Historically, most bullying took place at school, or between home and the school gates. As soon as a child got home they could shut the door behind them and find sanctuary. Home was a place where the bullies could not reach them. Mobile bullying has changed that.

A mobile phone is one of a child's most treasured personal possessions. They tend to keep it on all the time. So if the mobile starts being used to harass a child, be it through text or camera phone bullying, it can seem like there is no escape. The bullies always have a way of reaching them. They can feel trapped, with nowhere to hide and no one they can turn to for help. Or they might worry that if they do tell their parents or another adult, their mobile phone will be taken away from them.

### Putting U in the picture – key findings

A total of 770 youngsters aged 11 to 19 were questioned in the mobile bullying survey, which was carried out for NCH and Tesco Mobile by BMRB between 3 March and 6 April 2005.

---

*We define text bullying, the biggest mobile bullying problem, as one or more unwelcome text messages that the recipient finds threatening, or causes discomfort in some way*

---

*Question: Have you ever been bullied or threatened by someone using any of the following?*
One in five youngsters (20%) admitted they had experienced some sort of bullying or threat via email, Internet chat room or text. Some experienced more than one.

Text bullying was the most significant form of bullying at 14 per cent. This was followed by Internet chat rooms at 5 per cent and 4 per cent via email.

*Question: Using their mobile phone camera, has anybody ever taken a photograph of you in a way that made you feel uncomfortable, embarrassed or threatened?*
This question was new to the 2005 survey and the response was startling. One in 10 youngsters (10%) admitted this had happened to them – more than via email or Internet chat rooms.

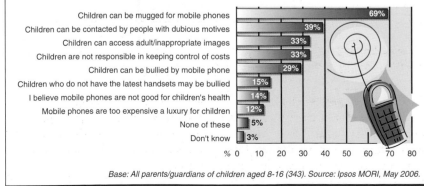

**Children and mobile phones**

Respondents were asked: 'On this card are a number of concerns about children aged 8 and upwards owning a mobile phone. Please tell me which two or three of these, if any, you personally are concerned about?'

| | % |
|---|---|
| Children can be mugged for mobile phones | 69% |
| Children can be contacted by people with dubious motives | 39% |
| Children can access adult/inappropriate images | 33% |
| Children are not responsible in keeping control of costs | 33% |
| Children can be bullied by mobile phone | 29% |
| Children who do not have the latest handsets may be bullied | 15% |
| I believe mobile phones are not good for children's health | 14% |
| Mobile phones are too expensive a luxury for children | 12% |
| None of these | 5% |
| Don't know | 3% |

% 0 10 20 30 40 50 60 70 80

*Base: All parents/guardians of children aged 8-16 (343). Source: Ipsos MORI, May 2006.*

Currently almost 4 million UK young people own a camera-enabled handset, with this figure set to double to 8 million by 2007.

**Question: As far as you know, was a photograph of that particular incident sent to anyone else?**

Of the young people who had had a photo taken that made them feel uncomfortable, embarrassed or threatened, 17 per cent believed the image had been sent to someone else.

**Question: Who was the bullying or threatening behaviour carried out by?**

Three-quarters (73%) of young people who had been bullied or threatened said they knew the person who bullied or threatened them, while a quarter (26%) said it was a stranger.

**Question: Did you tell anyone you had been bullied?**

Worryingly, more than a quarter of respondents (28%) did not tell anyone. Two-fifths (41%) of those bullied told a friend. A quarter (24%) spoke to a parent about it and 14 per cent to a teacher.

**Question: Would you say that you have ever sent a bullying or threatening message to someone else?**

One in 10 youngsters (11%) admitted they had sent a bullying or threatening message to someone else. A total of 87 per cent said no.

---

*Three-quarters (73%) of young people who had been bullied or threatened said they knew the person who bullied or threatened them*

---

**Question: Why did you not tell anyone that you had been bullied or threatened?**

Of the 28 per cent of respondents who were bullied or threatened but did not tell anyone, the majority (31%) said this was because 'it wasn't a problem'. A total of 12 per cent said it was because 'there was no one

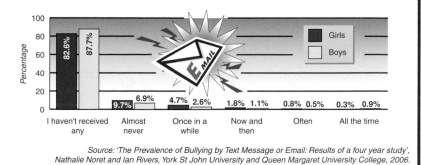

## Threatening texts and emails

**Percentage of pupils receiving nasty/threatening texts/emails.**

Source: 'The Prevalence of Bullying by Text Message or Email: Results of a four year study', Nathalie Noret and Ian Rivers, York St John University and Queen Margaret University College, 2006.

I wanted to tell', 11 per cent didn't think it would stop the bullying or threats and one in 10 (10%) didn't know where to go for help.

**Question: What kind of help or support would have encouraged you to report the threats or bullying?**

Of the 28 per cent of youngsters who were bullied or threatened but did not tell anyone, a quarter (23%) felt that 'knowing how to get hold of and speak to someone who was an expert at dealing with bullies' would have made a difference. A total of 15 per cent said 'knowing there was a staff member in my school/college dedicated to stopping bullying' would have helped. 'Knowing of a website with lots of advice and tips on dealing with bullies' was the next most popular answer at 13 per cent.

**Question: When did the threats or bullying take place?**

For youngsters in education, half (50%) of the threats or bullying happened at school or college. A total of 17 per cent took place at the weekend, 21 per cent after school or college and 6 per cent in the school/college holidays.

For those respondents not at school or college who had been bullied or threatened, 42 per cent said this happened after 9pm, 41 per cent between 9am and 6pm and 18 per cent between 6pm and 9pm.

## What are NCH and Tesco Mobile doing to tackle mobile bullying?

As the survey results clearly show, too many children are suffering in silence. NCH and Tesco Mobile are working together to make sure as many children as possible have access to information and advice

about how to deal with being bullied by mobile phone.

For this reason NCH and Tesco Mobile are launching an interactive website so young people can access information and advice about mobile bullying at the click of a button. The website – www.stoptextbully. com – will encourage youngsters to talk to an adult or friend about being bullied by mobile phone. It will also be a comprehensive guide full of information about where they can go for more help and advice.

A new 24-hour service is also being launched, where youngsters can text a special number if they are being bullied by mobile phone. All they need to do is text the word 'bully' to '60000' to receive more advice and support. Tesco Mobile will donate the cost of every text sent to this information service to NCH. That way every penny will help continue the battle against mobile bullying.

NCH and Tesco Mobile are also working closely with Tesco's Computers For Schools campaign. To help tackle mobile bullying, information will be sent to more than 28,000 schools across Britain, providing teachers, parents and guardians with the information they need to provide support to young people.

This is just the start of a longer term joint campaign to stamp out mobile bullying and prevent more children's lives being ruined.

■ The above information is reprinted with kind permission from NCH and Tesco Mobile. Visit www.stoptextbully.com for more information.

© NCH and Tesco Mobile

# stoptextbully top ten tips

## Information from NCH

1. Always tell someone you trust what's happening – this could be your parents, carer, teacher or friend. This might help you feel better and the person may also be able to help you to find a way to stop it altogether.

2. You may need to tell the local police. It's against the law to make a call or send a text or email that's really abusive or menacing, or to keep sending messages that will annoy someone or make them anxious. The sender could get fined or even go to prison!

---

*Never reply to the bully or send an even nastier message back. Often bullies will send a message to get a reaction, so don't respond to it*

---

3. Never reply to the bully or send an even nastier message back. Often bullies will send a message to get a reaction, so don't respond to it. Bullies who don't get a reaction often get bored and stop.

4. Keep and save messages. If there's a website, online voting site, weblog or message board that says bad things about you, save a copy

or print it off. The Internet service provider (ISP) that hosts the site should have an email address or helpline where you can send the copy and ask them to get rid of it. It might be a good idea to ask a trusted adult to help you contact the ISP.

5. Take a break from your phone or computer for a few days! Let your phone take messages and don't chat or check texts or emails. If you really need to make calls, find out if your phone can turn off incoming texts for a while. The bully might just get bored and stop.

6. Make sure only good friends and family are in your phone or email address book. If you don't recognise a number, caller ID or email, leave it and get a trusted adult to check it later.

7. If you really like using a chat room, you could sign up again with a different chat ID – use a nickname and don't give out any of your personal info. Hold back for a bit in the chat room until you're sure the bully's gone.

8. Always be careful who you give or lend your mobile to and always be careful about giving out your mobile phone number, especially if you change it – never give out your number in an Internet chat room. You don't know who else might be online and watching.

9. Your mobile phone provider can help you by changing your number if you start getting bullied through your phone.

10. Keep telling yourself: 'This bullying is wrong. It's not my fault and I'm not putting up with it!' You are not alone.

■ The above information is reprinted with kind permission from NCH. Visit www.stoptextbully.com for more information.

© NCH

# Mobile phone bullying

## Three-quarters of teachers are worried about mobile phone bullying

Nearly three quarters of teachers (74.4%) throughout the UK are worried that their pupils could become victims of mobile phone bullying, reveals research by leading children's charity NCH and Tesco Mobile released today (22 November 2005).

Worryingly, parents are still unsure about the issue, with nearly one in five parents (19%) thinking bullying by mobile phone is not common or never happens. This is despite research for NCH and Tesco Mobile which found that one in five young people have been bullied or threatened by mobile phone or computer.

The second stage of NCH and Tesco Mobile's 'Putting U in the Picture' campaign is focusing on adults' understanding of the issue. Teachers, parents and carers play an integral part in young people's lives and while teachers are concerned about mobile phone bullying, parents are unsure what is happening. Research has found more than half of the parents surveyed (56%) are not worried their child could be bullied or threatened by a mobile phone or are not sure how serious the issue is.

Top 20 teenage pop group Love Bites is supporting the campaign. The group is aged between 15 and 18 and have personal experiences of mobile phone and other types of bullying. They are available for photos and interviews at Mount Carmel School in Islington, London, N19 on Tuesday 22 November from 2pm. They will further support the campaign by performing to students from 2.30pm.

The research also reveals that:

- 51% of teachers know at least one of their pupils has been bullied or threatened by mobile phone. More than two-thirds of these (67%) were primary school teachers of children aged 11 and under;
- 73.2% of parents whose children had a mobile phone said their child had received it when they were aged between eight and 13;
- more than one-third of parents (36.5%) are not worried their child could be bullied or threatened by mobile phone;
- nearly three-quarters of teachers (74%) thought it was either common or very common for children to receive bullying or threatening messages via mobile phone text messaging;
- nearly 80% of teachers had been approached by a pupil or parent worried about bullying.

NCH's New Technology Adviser John Carr says: 'Technology is great for young people in so many ways but it also carries risks, with one in five young people who have been affected by mobile phone or online bullying.'

---

### 51% of teachers know at least one of their pupils has been bullied or threatened by mobile phone

---

'Through a range of initiatives NCH helps tackle bullying. We need to ensure all teachers, youth workers, parents, carers and any other interested parties understand just how bullying works in the online environment. Mobile phone companies need to follow our lead and act responsibly to ensure the best possible technological solutions are in place to protect our young people from harm.'

NCH and Tesco Mobile's 'Putting U in the Picture' campaign is:

- calling on all schools to ensure their anti-bullying policies include bullying via mobile phone or computer;
- sending information packs to secondary schools across the UK, encouraging teachers to address the issue with students and their parents. The information packs include: an interactive classroom quiz; top 10 tips; a poster and more. The pack can be downloaded from www.stoptextbully.com.

Tesco Mobile Chief Executive Officer Andy Dewhurst commented: 'This latest research shows that teachers are very concerned about the growing problem of mobile bullying. This is why Tesco Mobile and NCH wanted to provide them with a practical solution for addressing this issue within the school environment.'

'Mobile phones are hugely important to young people today and can be really beneficial from both a social and safety point of view. However, with all new technologies comes some problems and we are working closely with NCH to make sure that those responsible for young people understand this issue and know how they can help those who are affected.'

Dr Mary Bousted, General Secretary of the Association of Teachers and Lecturers (ATL), said: 'The Association of Teachers and Lecturers abhors bullying in any shape or form, and supports the campaign to combat the psychological bullying associated with mobile phones, including text bullying and "happy slapping".

'Highly effective anti-bullying practice already exists in a large number of schools, and the recent *Steer Report* recommendation "that schools have a clear policy on the possession and use of mobile phones on the school site" must be implemented to ensure both pupils and teachers are supported and protected.'

*22 November 2005*

- The above information is reprinted with kind permission from NCH. Visit www.nch.org.uk for more information.

© NCH

# Concern over rise of 'happy slapping' craze

## Fad of filming violent attacks on mobile phones spreads

In one video clip, labelled Bitch Slap, a youth approaches a woman at a bus stop and punches her in the face. In another, Knockout Punch, a group of boys wearing uniforms are shown leading another boy across an unidentified school playground before flooring him with a single blow to the head.

In a third, Bank Job, a teenager is seen assaulting a hole-in-the-wall customer while another youth grabs the money he has just withdrawn from the cash machine.

Welcome to the disturbing world of the 'happy slappers' – a youth craze in which groups of teenagers armed with camera phones slap or mug unsuspecting children or passersby while capturing the attacks on 3G technology.

According to police and anti-bullying organisations, the fad, which began as a craze on the UK garage music scene before catching on in school playgrounds across the capital last autumn, is now a nationwide phenomenon.

And as the craze has spread from London to the home counties to the north of England, so the attacks have become more menacing, with increasing numbers of violent assaults and adult victims.

In London, British Transport Police has investigated 200 happy slapping incidents in the past six months, with eight people charged with attacks at south London stations and bus stops in January alone.

The Metropolitan Police has no overall figures but recorded a number of attacks in London boroughs earlier this year.

Following a spate of random attacks last December on pupils at Godolphin and Latymer girls' school in Hammersmith, west London, police posted extra officers in the area as a deterrent.

But as police have become more vigilant, so the gangs have become more sophisticated, seeking victims in parks or public areas where their crimes are unlikely to be spotted by the authorities or captured on CCTV.

Liz Carnell, the director of Bullying Online, a Yorkshire-based charity set up to combat bullying in schools, said that since the start of the year she has heard of increasing attacks both on children and on adults. But she fears many incidents are not reported.

---

### Many victims do not realise they have been happy slapped until after the event

---

'In most cases the worst that happens is a minor scratch or a bruised ego,' she said.

'What the people behind these attacks have to understand is that technically they are committing an assault. And if they then upload the images on to the Internet or a phone system they could be prosecuted for harassment.'

What makes the attacks all the more bewildering is that many victims do not realise they have been happy slapped until after the event.

Earlier this month James Silver, 34, a freelance journalist, was attacked while jogging on the South Bank in London. While one youth blocked his path, another hit him with a rolled-up magazine.

When he spun around another teenager – who had been hiding behind nearby scaffolding – leapt out and hit him hard in the head.

When he staggered to his feet he noticed the rest of the gang were jeering and pointing their mobile phones at him.

Silver admits that while the attack left his 'ego smarting' he did not think it worth reporting. 'At the end of the day I was unharmed but it was pretty shocking at the time,' he said. 'The worry is that while the bulk of the attacks are trivial, some of these youths could be carrying knives.'

Earlier this year, schools in Lewisham, south London, and St Albans banned camera phones because of worries that the fad was leading to an increase in playground bullying.

In a comment recently posted on a London community web forum, 'Happyslapper2' described the craze as a 'joke', writing: 'If you feel bored wen ur about an u got a video phone den bitch slap sum norman, innit.'

However, in a sign of a gathering backlash, other forum members disagreed. 'It's hardly a joke ... it's fuckin rude and pea-brained,' wrote 'slappersidiots'.

'If this happy slapping fad continues it will only be a matter of time before someone is seriously hurt,' predicted another.

26 April 2005

# Bullying at work

**Bullying doesn't only happen to schoolkids, it shows its ugly face in the workplace too**

Harassment, intimidation and aggression are sometimes built into a company's management scheme, or may be carried out by just one individual. Bullying is a gradual process that wears the victim down, and makes them feel worthless, both as a worker and as a person.

### What is it?

The Andrea Adams Trust, the national charity against workplace bullying, defines it as:

- unnecessary, offensive, humiliating behaviour towards an individual or groups of employees;
- persistent, negative malicious attacks on personal or professional performance, often unpredictable and unfair or irrational;
- an abuse of power or position that can cause anxiety and distress, or physical ill health.

It can take obvious forms, such as physical violence or shouting and swearing, or be subtler, such as ignoring someone, giving them impossible tasks or encouraging malicious gossip about them. Being the best employee in the company is no protection; it may make you the target of a jealous person.

Employees often put up with bullying behaviour because they are afraid of losing their jobs, or think that complaining will make the situation worse.

### Here's 10 steps you can take to fight it

1. Deflect the bully if you can. Remain calm, stand firm, and try to keep up a confident appearance. Keep a detailed record of every incident; you will need it as proof if you decide to make a complaint.

2. Check your job description. If you suddenly find yourself being set menial tasks, or are given an increased workload with shorter deadlines, and it isn't in your contract then you can do something about it.
3. Try to get witnesses to bullying incidents, and avoid situations where you are alone with the bully.
4. Get advice from your trade union, or from personnel and health and safety officers at work. Does your employer have a policy on harassment or against unacceptable behaviour?
5. Take a stress management course, and do some assertiveness training. They are good for your general health, and will help you in the future.

6. If you go ahead with a complaint, choose your words carefully. State the facts clearly, but don't get sucked into a slanging match – you could be accused of malicious behaviour.
7. Get emotional support from your family and friends, talk to them about how you are feeling. Ask your GP about counselling. Take sick leave if you need it.
8. If you decide to leave your job because of the bullying, let your company know exactly why you are resigning. It may help others in the future.
9. If you wish to pursue a legal claim against your employer, start by taking advice from your union. If you have a good case, they will take it up on your behalf.
10. Many forms of legal action may be possible, including: industrial tribunals, civil claims for personal injury, and sometimes even criminal action.

- The above information is reprinted with kind permission from TheSite.org. Visit www.thesite.org for more information.

© TheSite.org

# How to deal with bullying at work

## Information from Mind

*'I used to be known as a confident high-flyer, but since he took over I know my confidence has been undermined and I feel under stress at work. He just picks on me constantly; it seems nothing I ever do is right. I am just always depressed, both at work and at home now. It really can't go on, but what can I do? I need this job.'*

*'Going to work suddenly seems like entering a war zone without a weapon. I think I am being bullied, but surely bullying stops at the school gates, doesn't it?'*

*'The thought of having to get up to go to work causes me such panic and fear that I am physically sick.'*

Bullying at work is a much greater problem than people once realised. It's bad for the individuals and for the organisations they work for. But it's a problem that can be difficult to identify and tackle. This booklet explains how and why bullying takes place, and what can be done about it. It also suggests where you can find further information and advice.

### What is workplace bullying?

Bullying behaviour is not about being bossy. It's not about the occasional, angry outburst on the subject of meeting work targets or reaching and maintaining standards. It's about persistent criticism and condemnation.

If you tell someone often enough that they are stupid, hopeless and not up to the job, they are likely to start believing it, and to imagine that it's entirely their own fault.

Workplace bullying is offensive discrimination, through persistent, vindictive, cruel or humiliating attempts to hurt, criticise and condemn an individual or a group of employees. It means the bully is abusing his or her power or position to:

## For better mental health

- undermine an individual's ability, causing them to lose their self-confidence and self-esteem;
- intimidate someone in a way that makes him or her feel very vulnerable, alone, angry and powerless.

These attacks on someone's performance are unpredictable, unreasonable and often unseen, typically. It's been likened to a cancer that creeps up on the person long before they are aware of what's happening. It wears the employee down, making them feel belittled and inadequate, and gradually makes them lose faith in themselves. It causes constant stress and anxiety, which can cause ill-health and mental distress.

### Why is it so hard to recognise?

This is a major problem, because bullying is rarely confined to obviously unkind remarks or open aggression. Covert bullying is hidden bullying: underhand, and difficult to confront, especially if your confidence and self-esteem is already undermined by it. Because it's so difficult to identify in the workplace, it requires much more investigation.

Most bullying at work is not blatant physical violence, but psychological violence. It's a hidden, yet repetitive progression of small events and persistent harassment.

It can take on a perfectly innocent appearance. For example, it may be an apparently harmless joke, at your expense. If you object, the bully may accuse you of having no sense of humour, or of taking things too seriously. Such incidents have a drip, drip effect.

Open bullying might consist of:

- physical violence;
- shouting or swearing at you, in public or private;

- instant rages over trivial matters;
- humiliating you in front of colleagues;
- deliberately ignoring or isolating you in public;
- taking disciplinary action out of the blue;
- never listening to your point of view;
- labelling you or calling you names;
- personal insults or ridicule;
- sarcasm;
- smear campaigns.

Covert bullying might include:

- constantly undervaluing your efforts
- persistent criticism;
- setting deadlines or objectives that are impossible to achieve;

- moving the goal posts;
- withholding information and blaming you for being ignorant;
- spreading malicious, unfounded rumours;
- ignoring, excluding and isolating you;
- making threats;
- removing areas of responsibility for no real reason;
- giving you menial or trivial tasks;
- stealing your ideas and taking credit for your achievements;
- giving you too little or too much work;
- blocking promotion;
- refusing reasonable requests for holidays or for training;
- constantly overruling your authority;
- monitoring everything you do
- blaming you whenever things go wrong.

---

*Bullying can sometimes be quite unconscious. The bully may be unaware of his or her own motives and of the full effects of their behaviour*

---

A bully will usually combine various types of behaviour. Over time, being on the receiving end of these tactics can amount to torture, making grown men and women weep, and fracturing careers. Bullying can sometimes be quite unconscious. The bully may be unaware of his or her own motives and of the full effects of their behaviour, and you may not pinpoint why your morale is so low. But if the bully is aware of causing you offence, he or she may see it as strong management or positive hands-on supervision. If they are constantly and vindictively picking on you, and disguising this from other people, the bullying is deliberate. In the end, whether or not they consciously intended to be hurtful is irrelevant. What counts is whether their behaviour is acceptable by normal standards, and whether it disadvantages you.

## Why do people become bullies?

Bullying is a basic human impulse, and can occur whenever people interact in some way. The behaviour crosses gender, age, colour and race. There's no typical bully, and bullying isn't connected to a particular personality type or to fixed ways of behaving at work. Each case of bullying is different, and takes place within a complex web formed by the personalities, the psychology, the organisation and the wider context involved.

There are any number of reasons why people might use bullying at work, but what shows up clearly across a number of studies is that bullies have a great need to control other people, either openly or indirectly. Most bullies are in positions of authority, as managers or supervisors. It may be that they are driven by envy and insecurity about their own competence, and that this emerges in their desire to keep any possible rivals down.

Bullying is essentially cowardly. The bully hides his or her own inadequacies, while making out that other people are at fault. The bully may see the other person as more capable, successful, popular or attractive than they are. The targets of bullying are usually above-average performers, much more efficient and better at what they do than the bully. This reason stands head and shoulders above all others for why certain people are targeted. Less common reasons include race, gender or disability, being vulnerable, timid or unassertive, or blowing the whistle on unacceptable working practices – including bullying.

## How can I know whether I'm being bullied?

Ask yourself the following questions.
- Does the working relationship feel different from any you have previously experienced?
- Are you being 'got at', constantly?
- Is your work being criticised, even though you know that your standards haven't slipped?
- Are you beginning to question whether the mistakes you're supposed to have made really are your fault?

If this is an accurate picture of what is happening to you at work, and it wasn't true before, ask yourself what has changed.
- Do you have a new boss?
- Has the pressure on your current boss increased?
- Have you recently changed jobs?
- Are your objectives always being changed?
- Are you under more personal scrutiny?
- Are you feeling less involved?
- Are you being asked to perform roles outside your job description?

## How does it differ from strong management?

Someone who is bossy or domineering is certainly being aggressive, but he or she will take responsibility for their actions and its consequences, in such a way that other people can comfortably deal with its effect. Providing the bossiness does not interfere with anybody else's rights and wellbeing, it's legitimate. But it's rather an ineffective and short-lived use of power. Although bullying is not the same as strong management, it often spreads downwards from a senior manager taking what they feel is a 'strong line' with employees. All managers have the right to manage, and are given the authority to do so. But they need to ask themselves the following questions:
- Is the criticism constructive or destructive?
- Is the criticism about the mistake, or about the person?

- Is it designed to make the person aware of their error and to get it right in future, or just to humiliate them?

You cross the line between strong management and bullying when there is a purposeful, malicious intent. It happens when hurting an employee or colleague by intimidating, upsetting, embarrassing, humiliating, offending or ultimately destroying them is more important than getting the task done. Bullying can easily become part of the culture in companies that pride themselves on their strong, robust management. Employees may assume that management allows and even condones such behaviour unless it takes action against it. Certain organisations are more likely to nurture bullying behaviour. These include places that are fiercely competitive, where there's fear of redundancy, where people lack proper training, where there are poor working relationships, where management is authoritarian and where there's little consultation and no accepted codes of conduct.

## What is harassment?

To all intents and purposes, bullying and harassment are the same things, because harassment means continuously troubling or annoying someone. However, we tend to attach the word harassment to conduct that focuses on particular aspects of a person – their state of mental health, for instance, or their race, colour, nationality, gender, sexual orientation, physical health, disability, impairment, beliefs or age.

In particularly nasty forms, this type of harassment can take the form of physical contact, obscene remarks and gestures, gossip, pressure to provide sexual favours, intrusion by pestering, spying and stalking, or even physical attacks.

## What are the effects of bullying?

The stress on people who are slowly and persistently undermined can cause physical and emotional symptoms. This often happens if their complaints about ill-treatment are not taken seriously. They are then left feeling angry and with a strong sense of injustice.

### How do organisations deal with bullying?

All respondents were asked 'How does your organisation deal with bullying?'

Bullying is dealt with through formal grievance procedures 30.6%

Specific policies and procedures to deal with bullying 25.2%

Don't know 44.2%

Source: Digital Opinion. From the National Workplace Bullying Survey 2005-2006.

As a rule, bullying is not a subject that's readily discussed among colleagues, even though it might be happening to a number of people in the same workplace. If someone believes they alone have been singled out for attack, they can end up feeling it's their own fault. This can happens even when their work record was unblemished until there was a sudden (and relevant) change in circumstances – the arrival of a new boss or a change of management. In accepting the blame, their self-confidence crumbles and this inevitably undermines their performance. In these circumstances, people may well start taking time off work.

---

*The stress on people who are slowly and persistently undermined can cause physical and emotional symptoms*

---

Bullying brings unimagined misery, with consequences that may be tragic. There are documented cases of people's physical health being damaged, and many more cases involving psychological distress, breakdown of mental health, or personality change. And this is in addition to the financial problems people may have to face and the disruption to their career. Bullying can also devastate family life. Relationships deteriorate, children get less attention, and divorce rates increase.

Bullying can provoke the following symptoms:

- backache;
- severe headaches;
- sleeplessness;
- feeling sick;
- sweating and shaking;
- palpitations;
- excessive thirst;
- constant tiredness;
- skin complaints;
- loss of appetite;
- stomach problems;
- acute anxiety;
- panic attacks;
- irritability;
- mood swings;
- tearfulness;
- loss of interest in sex;
- loss of self-esteem;
- lack of motivation;
- obsessiveness and withdrawal;
- depression;
- suicidal thoughts.

Persistent, unpredictable bullying creates such fear that individuals frequently make up reasons for staying away from work. They can also develop feelings of paranoia, believing that if they tell tales, the bully will pursue them. If no one officially acknowledges what they are going through, most people being bullied will admit to having murderous feelings towards the person who is making their lives a misery. Targets of bullying devote a great deal of time to imagining how they might get rid of their tormentor. Such fantasies are common, and provide an outlet. But, unfortunately, the aggression can turn inwards, and may result in attempted sucide.

- Reprinted from 'How to deal with bullying at work' by permission of Mind (National Association for Mental Health – www.mind.org.uk).

© 2004 Mind

# Workplace bullying

## Information from the Trades Union Congress

### How common is bullying at work?

As many as one in 10 people were bullied at work over the past six months, or around 2 million of the UK's 24 million employees.

This evidence is from *Destructive Conflict*, the UK's largest-ever study of workplace bullying. Many 'targets' of bullying say they are being victimised on a daily or weekly basis.

---

*People who are bullied often lose self-confidence, perhaps for a long time, and suffer from work-related stress*

---

A trade union survey by Unison of workers in local government and the health service found that:

- nearly one worker in five (18%) was bullied in the past six months;
- anger, stress and powerlessness were the most common reactions;
- in terms of their position, more than eight bullies in 10 were managers.

### How can bullying affect me?

Bullying can make you ill, lose sleep, and make you dread the next day at work.

People who are bullied often lose self-confidence, perhaps for a long time, and suffer from work-related stress. And stress, in turn, causes ill-health, both physical and mental.

These are some of the ill-health symptoms of bullying:

*Your body*

- Headaches/migraine.
- Sweating/shaking.
- Feeling or being sick.
- Irritable bowel.
- Inability to sleep and loss of appetite.

*Your state of mind*

- Anxiety.
- Panic attacks.
- Depression.
- Tearfulness.

*Your behaviour*

- Becoming irritable.
- Becoming withdrawn.
- Increased consumption of tobacco, alcohol, etc.
- Obsessive dwelling on the bully, and seeking justice or revenge.

### Where do bullies flourish?

In organisations that fail to distinguish between 'managing' and 'bullying'. It can happen in large and small organisations, and in so-called 'caring professions'.

The personality 'defects' of a bully, such as aggressiveness, sarcasm, anger and maliciousness, flourish in certain kinds of work culture:

- in highly competitive or macho environments;
- in organisations undergoing radical change, or serious cuts;
- in a climate of job insecurity, e.g. redundancy;
- under 'tough' and hierarchical styles of management;
- where there's a lack of staff consultation;
- where excessive demands are made on people;
- where no procedures exist to tackle bullying.

### What can I do to tackle a bully?

Whatever steps you decide to take, you have the right to work in a safe environment. This includes not being harassed or bullied by anyone. You should not have to suffer in silence.

Confronting a bully yourself is not easy. It's probably only effective in its early stages. Often, the bully is a manager, so you need to get good, confidential advice on what to do.

These suggestions are drawn from the experience of people who have suffered from bullying, and from union and voluntary sector advice. We suggest you read through the sections below and think things over before deciding where to start.

*Talk to someone – get advice*

- Talk to someone you feel you can trust. This helps overcome the feeling of isolation and helplessness you may well be experiencing.

## Actions taken against workplace bullying

**What did you do when you experienced workplace bullying?**

| Action | % |
|---|---|
| Talked with family or friends | 74.6% |
| Talked with colleagues | 58.2% |
| Started looking for another job | 52.8% |
| Saw a doctor | 49.2% |
| Spoke with senior manager | 39.7% |
| Spoke with HR (Personnel) | 35.3% |
| Made an informal complaint | 35.1% |
| Spoke with union/staff assoc. | 34.8% |
| Confronted the bully | 33.6% |
| Made a formal complaint | 32.4% |
| Spoke with immediate manager | 31.9% |
| Took legal advice | 22.1% |
| Other | 16.7% |
| Contacted an external agency | 12.4% |

*Source: Digital Opinion. From the National Workplace Bullying Survey 2005-2006.*

- Visit your GP. Make an appointment with your doctor if you are experiencing ill-health symptoms of bullying.
- If you are a union member, talk to your union rep in confidence. Union reps should be able to advise you, know the right procedures, and help you deal with it, formally or informally.
- Contact a voluntary organisation or helpline. The Andrea Adams Trust or the Suzy Lamplugh Trust give free, confidential help and advice on bullying.
- Some employers nominate 'harassment advisers'. These fellow workers support and provide confidential advice to victims of bullying.

---

*Try talking to the bully. But if you decide to do so, then first of all go over what you want to say with someone else who understands what you are going through*

---

- Use an employee helpline. Some employers and unions operate free, confidential advice lines.
- Keep a record or diary. Record the date/time/place of important incidents, abuse, accusations, changes to your job. Keep copies of relevant letters, memos and appraisals.

*Be better informed – get a copy of:*
- your employer's anti-bullying or grievance procedure – it may be in the staff handbook;
- one of the anti-bullying handbooks we recommend in the TUC handbook, *Keeping Well At Work*, which also gives examples of how people coped with bullying.

*Take action*
- Try talking to the bully. But if you decide to do so, then first of all go over what you want to say with someone else who understands what you are going through.

- Have a clear idea of what you would expect to happen. Then, tell the bully how you find their behaviour unacceptable. Describe its effect on you. Make a note of this meeting, who said what and the outcome. If this informal approach doesn't work,

there are other formal options to use later.
- Make a formal complaint. Be well prepared. Familiarise yourself with your employer's procedures. Get a copy of your job description if you believe your harassment includes changes to your main responsibilities.
- Use your right to be accompanied at any meeting. Take a companion of your choice (fellow worker or someone outside) with you in any grievance hearing. This includes meetings with management on bullying.

- The above information is reprinted with kind permission from the Trades Union Congress. Visit www.worksmart.org.uk for more information.

© TUC

---

# If you're being bullied

## Information from the Andrea Adams Trust

1. Find out if your employer has a policy and procedures on harassment and bullying and obtain a copy.
2. Stand calm and firm and do not allow yourself to be a target.
3. Do not become isolated, seek immediate support and advice.
4. Keep a record of all incidents which cause you distress or are undermining – log dates and details and write down your feelings after each such occurrence together with your own response.
5. Try to get witnesses to bullying incidents by avoiding situations where you are alone with the bully.
6. Do not take action alone. Make an appointment with your company harassment advisor and seek their guidance and support.
7. Talk to colleagues and see if they are experiencing the same treatment as you.
8. Follow the company grievance procedures with the help and support of your harassment advisor, personnel or union officers.
9. Keep your complaint as objective as possible so that you can't be accused of filing the complaint out of malice or ambition.
10. Make an appointment with your doctor and tell them what is happening to you at work. Follow medical instructions and get signed off if necessary.
11. If counselling is available at work make an early appointment to talk through your experience.
12. Talk to friends and family for emotional support.
13. Get in touch with the Andrea Adams Trust Helpline: 01273 704900.

- The above information is reprinted with kind permission from the Andrea Adams Trust. Visit www.banbullyingatwork.com for more information.

© Andrea Adams Trust

# National workplace bullying survey

## The feedback

**W**elcome to the National Workplace Bullying Survey's report. Jointly run by the Andrea Adams Trust and Digital Opinion, it was the UK's most comprehensive ongoing survey into workplace bullying, and was open to anyone who considers themselves to have been a victim. With seven key questions, it was a simplified version of our Organisational Bullying Survey which explores this complex issue in much more depth.

### Summary

The report is based on all the responses (3,235) received since the launch of the survey in mid-March 2005. It provides a view of workplace bullying from the perspective of the victim.[1]

---

*60% of respondents say that workplace bullying has affected the quality of their work, and 51% say that it has caused them to take time off*

---

The feedback indicates that workplace bullying is perpetrated by a range of individuals, from directors to reports, with immediate managers being cited most often. It takes a variety of forms. Unfair criticism and intimidating behaviour are the most commonly cited examples, while some respondents indicate that they have been the victims of physical abuse.

Just over half of victims of bullying said that they had been bullied for over a year. Almost 23% had been bullied for six to 12 months.

## digital opinion...
### ...how surveys can be

Workplace bullying affects people in different ways. The most commonly cited effects are worry about going to work, and a lowering of self-esteem and self-confidence. It also has an impact on performance. 60% of respondents say that it has affected the quality of their work, and 51% say that it has caused them to take time off.

People respond to workplace bullying in different ways. 75% say that they discussed it with family or friends, while 58% talked with colleagues. Just 32% made a formal complaint. 53% say that they started looking for another job and 22% took legal advice.

5% of respondents say that their actions solved the problem, while 31.5% say that they achieved a partial solution. Unfortunately, more than 38% say that their actions had no effect, while a quarter of victims say that they actually made the situation worse.

When asked about how their organisation deals with workplace bullying, 44% of respondents say they do not know, 25% say that their organisation has specific policies and procedures in place, while the rest say that it is dealt with through the normal grievance procedures.

*1. It should be noted that the responses to the survey are taken at face value. The views expressed are not corroborated.*

■ The above information is reprinted with kind permission from Digital Opinion. For more information, please visit their website at www.digitalopinion.co.uk

*© Digital Opinion*

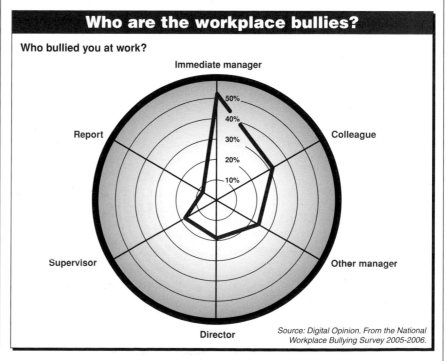

**Who are the workplace bullies?**

Who bullied you at work?

Immediate manager · Colleague · Other manager · Director · Supervisor · Report

*Source: Digital Opinion. From the National Workplace Bullying Survey 2005-2006.*

**Responses from the National Workplace Bullying Survey, conducted by Digital Opinion and the Andrea Adams Trust between March 2005 and May 2006.**

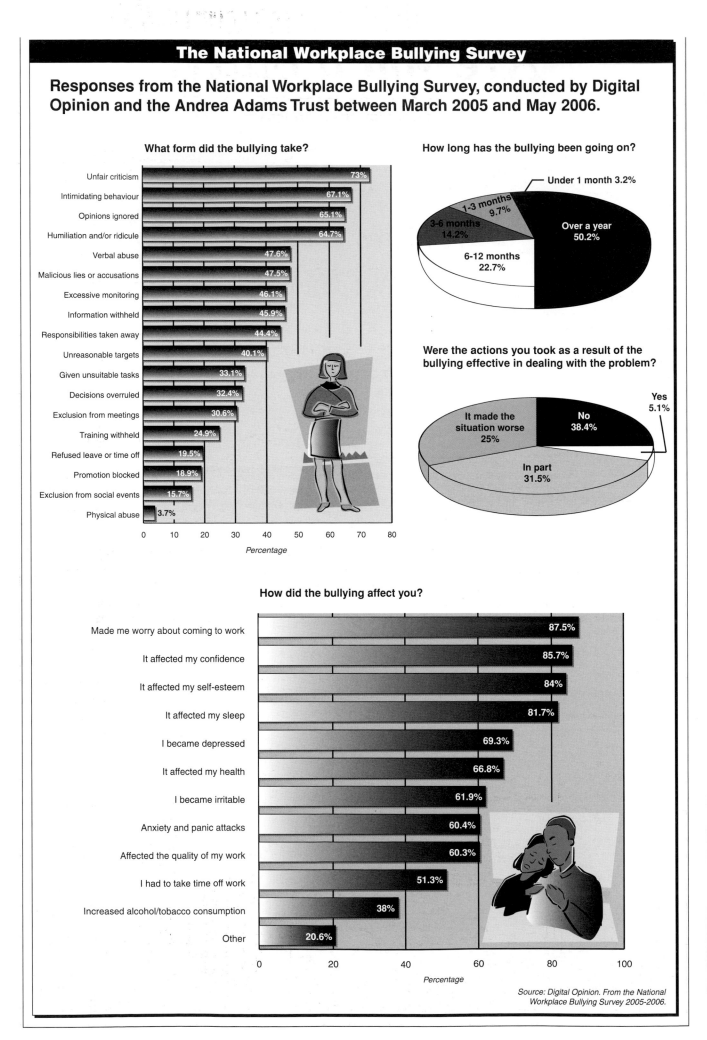

**What form did the bullying take?**

| Category | Percentage |
| --- | --- |
| Unfair criticism | 73% |
| Intimidating behaviour | 67.1% |
| Opinions ignored | 65.1% |
| Humiliation and/or ridicule | 64.7% |
| Verbal abuse | 47.6% |
| Malicious lies or accusations | 47.5% |
| Excessive monitoring | 46.1% |
| Information withheld | 45.9% |
| Responsibilities taken away | 44.4% |
| Unreasonable targets | 40.1% |
| Given unsuitable tasks | 33.1% |
| Decisions overruled | 32.4% |
| Exclusion from meetings | 30.6% |
| Training withheld | 24.9% |
| Refused leave or time off | 19.5% |
| Promotion blocked | 18.9% |
| Exclusion from social events | 15.7% |
| Physical abuse | 3.7% |

*Percentage*

**How long has the bullying been going on?**

- Under 1 month 3.2%
- 1-3 months 9.7%
- 3-6 months 14.2%
- 6-12 months 22.7%
- Over a year 50.2%

**Were the actions you took as a result of the bullying effective in dealing with the problem?**

- It made the situation worse 25%
- No 38.4%
- In part 31.5%
- Yes 5.1%

**How did the bullying affect you?**

| Category | Percentage |
| --- | --- |
| Made me worry about coming to work | 87.5% |
| It affected my confidence | 85.7% |
| It affected my self-esteem | 84% |
| It affected my sleep | 81.7% |
| I became depressed | 69.3% |
| It affected my health | 66.8% |
| I became irritable | 61.9% |
| Anxiety and panic attacks | 60.4% |
| Affected the quality of my work | 60.3% |
| I had to take time off work | 51.3% |
| Increased alcohol/tobacco consumption | 38% |
| Other | 20.6% |

*Percentage*

*Source: Digital Opinion. From the National Workplace Bullying Survey 2005-2006.*

# Are you a bully?

## Information from Amicus

**W**ith research showing that almost 80% of managers admit that bullying occurs in their organisations, could you be called a bully? Check out our suggestions on how to turn bullying behaviour into best practice.

### Firm but fair

Being a boss isn't a popularity contest. Everyone needs a telling off at some point. Do not scold people severely with a dressing down; just make your point firmly without intimidating or frightening your employees.

> *Being a boss isn't a popularity contest. Everyone needs a telling off at some point*

### Take a deep breath

Don't shout every time you feel the temperature rising. Do your best to restrain yourself and take a step back. If you get a reputation as a tantrum king or queen then you will automatically get the bully label.

### Communicate

Find time to sit down and communicate with your team or assistant, no matter how busy you are. Thrash-

*amicus the union*

ing out the week's priorities over a coffee will reduce stress levels and any potential conflict when the going gets tough.

### Measure yourself

If you have a problem with one of your team then address it in the right manner. Do not rant or bitch about their shortcomings behind their back as this will undermine them and ultimately make them feel inferior and excluded. It might also make them a target for others.

### Keep a level playing field

While people deserve praise when they have done a good job, make sure you play fair. Letting 'favourites' develop is a dangerous game that can upset office politics and make people feel excluded.

### Don't be a mirror

If you don't like the way your boss treats you, don't act like them. Think about how you feel when someone treats you badly. Just because you've

been managed badly, doesn't mean you have the right to dish it out further down the line.

### Listen to ideas

If someone challenges you, don't bite their head off. Think about what they have to say, make a note and let them know how their idea may work next time.

### Don't leave people out

When you organise the company get-together, make sure everyone is involved. Try and encourage everyone to attend if they can, and don't let anyone feel that they are being excluded or left out.

■ The above information is reprinted with kind permission from Amicus. Visit www.dignityatwork.org for more information.

© Amicus

SHE'S YOUR BOSS?! -THOUGHT SHE WAS ONE OF THE TEAM...

-SHE IS!!

# Bullying: a big problem for small businesses?

## Information from the British Psychological Society

Employees who work in small and medium sized businesses may be less at risk of being bullied, but prevention of bullying remains necessary for potential victims, according to psychologists.

Previous research has consistently found less bullying in small and medium sized enterprises (SMEs) but no previous study has analysed specific aspects in SMEs that are related to the problem of bullying.

> *Employees who work in small and medium sized businesses may be less at risk of being bullied, but prevention of bullying remains necessary for potential victims, according to psychologists*

Inge Neyens and her colleagues at Katholieke Universiteit Leuven in Belgium tried to find possible task, team and organisational risk factors for bullying in SMEs. She will present her findings today, Thursday 15 September 2005, at the conference 'Working Together

The British Psychological Society

to Tackle Workplace Bullying: Concepts, Research and Solutions', which is being held at the University of Portsmouth.

The researchers questioned 368 people from 39 SMEs, which varied in their sector, size and geographical location. They found a high workload, high role conflict and lower use of skills related to personal and work-related bullying. The victims also reported that their team members engaged in less problem-solving when a conflict occurred.

The researchers also found employees with a tenure of one to five years or more than 25 years were more prone to become a victim of personal bullying, such as teasing or ridicule.

They also suggest workers in SMEs could be at risk of bullying because of organisational changes, the lack of a policy against bullying and because they are working in family businesses.

Ms Neyens said: 'To reduce personal and work-related bullying in SMEs, small organisations have to take care of the workload, role conflicts and skill utilisation of their employees. Also, promoting "problem solving" in teams as a way for dealing with conflicts could help to prevent bullying.

'Finally, although most employers and employees think a policy against bullying is not really needed, the results suggest that employees of organisations with such a policy report less bullying.'
*4 October 2005*

■ The above information is reprinted with kind permission from the British Psychological Society. Visit www.bps.org.uk for more information.

© *British Psychological Society*

# The bully at work: Jan's story

**Bullying is alive and well in the British workplace. Read about one woman's experience and find out what you can do if you're experiencing it at work. By Joan Kingsley**

*'The effects of bullying lead to a sense of helplessness, inadequacy, confusion, anxiety, tiredness, disorganisation at work, lowered self-esteem and depression.'*
Dr Maurice Lipsedge, Honorary Consultant Psychiatrist, Guy's Hospital

### What bullies do

*'I'd been with the company twelve years when my new director arrived. From day one she just didn't like me. It started with her trying to win over people's regard by embarrassing me at meetings.'*

Bullying is a deliberate attempt by a boss, colleague, or ambitious junior to control and undermine you. It is not a one-off incident; bullying occurs continually over a period of many months. Your self-confidence becomes eroded. That can happen pretty fast.

*'In front of my colleagues she'd say: "I have a problem with you, I can't rely on you." Privately, she'd hurl offensive verbal abuse at me.'*

The bully is likely to verbally mistreat you with accusations, admonitions and threats. You may be quietly mocked in front of colleagues, and subjected to explosive outbursts behind closed doors. You feel frightened, angry, ashamed and embarrassed.

*'I began to hear of meetings that I wasn't asked to attend. Emails relating to my work were circulated to everyone but me. Lame excuses were given and I didn't know what to believe or who to trust.'*

The bully may exclude you from the information loop and threaten your professional standing. You become isolated and suspicious.

*'She began to pile irrelevant work on my desk; the deadlines were impossible to meet.'*

The bully may attempt to wear you down with overwork and absurd expectations. You become overwrought, jittery, and overtired. You toss and turn all night, suffer from nightmares, and have trouble dragging yourself out of bed in the morning. Your stomach is in knots, you have frequent headaches, and lose your appetite.

*'I did everything to please her, but nothing was good enough. She criticised my manner, appearance and management of others – in fact, everything I did. Worst of all, she presented my ideas as her own.'*

The bully may accuse you of not trying hard enough, of producing poor-quality work, and of not pulling your weight. Your very presence may be under attack. You up your performance only to find the bully running with your ideas. You become paralysed with fear and question everything you do and say. The very thought of work fills you with dread.

*'She went around asking for evidence of my misdoings and making it clear that*

there would be rewards for spying on me. Everyone was anxious about their position and people started avoiding me. I became a bundle of nerves, couldn't sleep and found myself uncontrollably bursting into tears; I felt miserable and was severely depressed. It became a downward spiral and I couldn't see a way out.'*

The bully may use his or her position of power to personally destroy you. You feel helpless and hopeless and every aspect of your life is negatively impacted upon. You are convinced it's all your fault; that there must be something wrong with you.

### Why me?

*'I sought the help of the HR director but he told me it was my issue: "You're single, lonely, you can't fit in, you don't have many friends." I was devastated.'*

Bullying always feels personal because it always is personal. For the bully at work, you are not really a person with feelings but an object to be manipulated and manoeuvred against. The motivations may lie in the character and personal history of the bully or they may derive from a hidden organisational agenda. Whatever the reasons, bullying tactics are always an act of cowardice. But, as Dr Paul Brown, Director of Adaptive Research at Penna Holdings plc, says, 'The trouble is, it takes two to be bullied. The person who is being bullied begins to feel like the coward. It's a complete invasion.'

### What can you do?

1. Trust your instincts. If it feels like bullying, it most likely is.
2. Knowledge is power. Gather information. Has the bully done this before? Is fear running

rampant around this bully? Is this colleague willing to stamp on anyone in their quest for fame and fortune? Is there a hidden organisational agenda?

3. Consult the grapevine. Is this a new manager appointed to be the bearer of bad tidings and an agent of change? Has there been a restructuring due to a merger or acquisition? Is there takeover talk in the air? Is there any hint of downsizing and/or outsourcing? Keep your eyes focused on whispering corners. Keep you ears tuned in to potentially informative small talk.

---

*Keep a diary. What is called 'a contemporaneous record' is very much more powerful than half-remembered events later on if it comes to a real dispute with the organisation*

---

4. Keep a diary. What is called 'a contemporaneous record' is very much more powerful than half-remembered events later on if it comes to a real dispute with the organisation.

5. Find your voice. Write a memorandum to the bully setting out the criticisms concisely, coldly, and clearly. Request an immediate and detailed response to support the allegations. Send a copy to the Human Resources department and to relevant directors.

6. Stand up and be counted. Request that HR spell out organisational policy regarding bullying. Request that training seminars be instituted to counteract the effects of bullying. Petition colleagues for support.

### When the going gets tough?

*'I wrote letters to management and personnel and the responses were dire. I finally went to a psychologist who helped me tackle the situation from a business point of view. You need someone to tell you you're not wrong.'*

1. Get friendly help. Call on sympathetic friends who will listen and support you. Don't try to cope on your own.

2. Get professional help. Counsellors, psychotherapists, and psychologists can offer sound professional help and guidance. Ask your GP for a referral. You can get telephone numbers from the British Psychological Society, the UKCP (United Kingdom Council for Psychotherapy), and the BAC (British Association of Counsellors).

3. Knowing when to leave. With all the will in the world, some bullies are not worth the battle. Ask yourself why you'd want to stay in an organisation that runs on fear. If your bully is acting on an organisational agenda it's not a battle you can win in any event. As Jan discovered…

*'I'd worked in this business for 25 years and it takes a long time to realise you've got to go. The lawyer I finally saw said, 'You're not fighting for your job – that's gone – but for money. It's only about money.' Once I understood that, the rest was just about letting go and getting on with my life. Two years later I'm still bruised but happier than I've ever been.'*

■ The above information is reprinted with kind permission from iVillage UK. For more information, please visit their website at www.iVillage.co.uk.

© *iVillage*

---

# Mental toughness helps resist bullying

### Information from the British Psychological Society

**M**entally tough individuals report less bullying at work and show less mental distress.

That is the conclusion of Dr Iain Coyne of the Institute of Work, Health and Organisations, who presented his findings at the British Psychological Society's Division of Occupational Psychology Annual Conference on Friday 13 January 2006. The conference is taking place at the Crowne Plaza Glasgow (formerly Glasgow Moat House Hotel).

Together with his colleagues from the University of Hull, Dr Coyne surveyed 93 men and women, who were mainly employed in non-managerial positions, measuring their experiences of bullying over the last six months. They also rated their own psychological stress and completed a measure of mental toughness.

The research demonstrated that qualities, such as confidence and feelings of being in control, were clearly linked with lower reports of bullying and better psychological wellbeing.

Dr Coyne said: 'Mentally tough individuals tend to perceive stressors (such as bullying) as opportunities and will persist in the face of such threats. They tend to be confident and to feel that they are in control of their work environment. Given this, they are likely to have some resistance to the effects of the stressor.'

The findings of a further study of 36 students will also be presented. This work suggests that training in mental toughness may have the potential to help people cope with workplace bullying.

*13 January 2006*

■ The above information is reprinted with kind permission from the British Psychological Society. Visit www.bps.org.uk for more information.

© *British Psychological Society*

# Fear and loathing in the workplace

**It's bad enough that many employers turn a blind eye to the problem of bullying, says Roxanne Escobales. But could some even be encouraging such abuse?**

From the day Jane Black's new manager started, she knew something was not right. It wasn't until she came back from sick leave to find her desk, her computer and her phone had been taken away that she knew something was definitely wrong. She just didn't know what it was.

Black was being bullied. And she isn't the only one. New research published this month by the Chartered Management Institute (CMI) highlights the widespread nature of bullying in the workplace – 60% of managers in the UK think bullying is on the increase, yet the same amount reported that they had received no training on how to tackle it.

But the findings also indicate that this is a preventable problem. More than half of the managers who responded to the survey said their organisations had no formal policy on bullying. Without sanctioned procedures for investigating claims of workplace abuse, workers can often feel abandoned. HR departments, the research showed, find it difficult to address and correct bullying behaviour, and victims get no support, which increases their sense of helplessness.

Alongside the research, CMI has issued guidance to encourage businesses and organisations to develop policy to address this abuse of power. They urge companies to take responsibility for the behaviour of their employees, says the CMI chief executive, Mary Chapman.

'Our recommendation for developing a policy is not so much for the bit of paper that results, but for all those things that are done in thinking about the problem and coming up with ideas about how to address it,' she says.

As bullying contributes to stress, absenteeism and low morale which, in turn, results in reduced productivity, it is in an organisation's best interests to respond to the problem. Addressing the workplace culture is an important factor in this, says Dr Sandi Mann, an occupational psychologist and contributor to the research, because those likely to bully will thrive in an environment that encourages such behaviour.

Certain types of workplaces are more likely to foster – however unwittingly – this culture. Highly competitive industries, organisations that are going through radical change and where there is a climate of insecurity, and those with very hierarchical styles of management where there is little or no staff consultation, are prime examples.

Bullying in the office can take the form of obviously abusive actions such as shouting at employees or 'accidents' such as spilling coffee on someone else's work. But it can take more subtle forms as well. On one occasion, Black worked on a project for three weeks, but when her manager found one mistake in it he reassigned the project to a less experienced colleague, she recalls.

Other undermining practices can include setting unrealistic deadlines, refusing requests for leave or for training opportunities, and assigning the target the undesirable shifts on the rota.

Targets of bullying tend to be in vulnerable positions, such as working on short-term contracts, having low status or being from a minority group. Those who are shy, quiet, non-assertive and lack self-esteem may also suffer. 'But no one is immune,' Mann stresses.

In the five-and-a-half years since Black left her job, she has suffered severe depression and hair loss; she has even attempted suicide. She still feels the effects, although she says she has 'come to terms with it now'.

It wasn't until she found help through a bullying support group that she was able to break out of this cycle, which had seen her become a virtual recluse.

'To me, people who were bullied were safe, because I thought they weren't going to bully me,' she says. 'I couldn't go out and meet other people because I thought they would bully me. I couldn't discriminate.'

Last year she took her life back and joined an organisation that gives support, advice and information to those who have experienced workplace bullying. Instead of being a target, she is now the one who takes aim.

*Jane Black's name has been changed.*

*19 September 2005*

# KEY FACTS

■ Homophobic bullying has been reported in primary, as well as secondary schools. It may be directed at young people of any sexual orientation and at children who have not yet reached puberty. Teachers, parents and other adults in schools may also be bullied in this way. (page 3)

■ Bullying usually involves a person or group exploiting the fact that they feel more powerful than another. (page 5)

■ Bullies pick on easy targets, so poor posture and averted eye contact will attract unwanted attention. (page 5)

■ 52 per cent of children and young people say that bullying is a big problem in their school, according to a new survey for the Anti-Bullying Alliance – and the same number think that schools are not doing enough to tackle the issue. (page 7)

■ We all need self-esteem, and children are no different. Children who are feeling bad about themselves or going through a difficult time may try to become more confident through exercising power over others. (page 8)

■ Each week at least 450,000 young children are bullied at school. (page 11)

■ More than one in five severely bullied children will attempt to take their own life. (page 11)

■ A survey reveals that while two out of three girls admit abusing others, more than 90 per cent say they have been bullied themselves. (page 14)

■ Few bullies in a survey admitted to worrying about their behaviour, with one-third saying they 'felt fine' after bullying someone because 'they deserved it'. (page 14)

■ Research carried out by Parentline Plus found that bullying by girls is becoming more underhand with a devastating effect on the victims – increasing the risks of suicide and self-harm. (page 15)

■ Virtually every pupil in the country is affected by an epidemic of bullying in schools, the Government's 'children's tsar' has claimed. (page 17)

■ Recent research from Brunel University recommends a form of children's community service for bullies and shows that bullies learn from external role models (i.e. soap opera characters) as well as parents. (page 18)

■ The authors of a study surveyed 11,227 children for the last four years about their experiences of bullying. Nearly 15% said that they had received nasty or aggressive text messages or emails. And there is a steady year-on-year increase in the number of children who are being bullied using new technology. (page 20)

■ 29% of parents of 8 to 16 year olds surveyed by Ipsos MORI were concerned about bullying via mobile phone. (page 22)

■ One in 10 youngsters (11%) admitted they had sent a bullying/threatening message to someone else. (page 23)

■ Nearly three-quarters of teachers (74.4%) throughout the UK are worried that their pupils could become victims of mobile phone bullying. (page 25)

■ Most bullying at work is not blatant physical violence, but psychological violence. It's a hidden, yet repetitive progression of small events and persistent harassment. (page 28)

■ Bullying is a basic human impulse, and can occur whenever people interact in some way. The behaviour crosses gender, age, colour and race. (page 29)

■ Although bullying is not the same as strong management, it often spreads downwards from a senior manager taking what they feel is a 'strong line' with employees. (page 29)

■ According to the National Workplace Bullying Survey, most respondents (44.2%) were unaware of how their organisation dealt with bullying. (page 30)

■ A trade union survey by Unison of workers in local government and the health service found that nearly one worker in five (18%) was bullied in the past six months. (page 31)

■ Feedback from the National Workplace Bullying Survey indicates that workplace bullying is perpetrated by a range of individuals, from directors to reports, with immediate managers being cited most often. It takes a variety of forms. Unfair criticism and intimidating behaviour are the most commonly cited examples, while some respondents indicate that they have been the victims of physical abuse. (page 33)

■ Employees who work in small and medium-sized businesses may be less at risk of being bullied, but prevention of bullying remains necessary for potential victims, according to psychologists. (page 36)

■ Mentally tough individuals report less bullying at work and show less mental distress, according to Dr Iain Coyne of the Institute of Work, Health and Organisations. (page 38)

# GLOSSARY

**Anger management**
Techniques used to teach someone how to deal with their anger if they consistently find this to be beyond their control. These techniques are often useful in teaching bullies how to change their behaviour.

**Brat-bully**
A term coined with reference to a new breed of middle-class bullies who, it is claimed, are over-indulged at home and believe the world revolves around them.

**Bullying**
Bullying is when people deliberately hurt, harass or intimidate someone else. It can include name-calling, teasing, physical attacks, abusive text messages, phone calls or emails, rumour-spreading and gossip, deliberately ignoring someone and being attacked on the basis of race, religion, gender, appearance, sexuality, disability or ethnicity. Bullying can take place anywhere, but is often a particular problem in schools and workplaces. Every year, more than 20,000 young people call ChildLine about bullying.

**Cyberbullying**
Also called e-bullying. This uses new technology as a method of bullying – bullies may send threatening messages to a victim's mobile phone or email account, or via instant messaging. One in five children now report that they have been bullied in this way. It has also been known for some bullies to set up websites targeting an individual.

**'Happy slapping'**
A recent craze involving bullies taking pictures or video clips of physical attacks on victims using mobile phones, which they then send on or share via the Internet.

**Homophobic bullying**
Bullying of an individual because they are, or are perceived to be, gay or lesbian.

**'No-blame' policy**
A controversial anti-bullying policy employed by some schools, which uses methods such as support groups in order to attempt to get a bully to consider the consequences of their actions and change their behaviour. Some people disagree with this policy as they feel it allows bullies to effectively escape punishment, which can be frustrating for victims and their parents.

**Racist bullying**
Any hostile or offensive action against people because of skin colour, cultural/religious background or ethnic origin.

**Workplace bullying**
Offensive discrimination, through persistent, vindictive, cruel or humiliating attempts to hurt, criticise and condemn an individual or a group of employees. It means the bully is abusing his or her position to undermine an individual's ability and intimidate them. As many as one in ten people were bullied at work over the past six months.

# INDEX

# ADDITIONAL RESOURCES

## Other Issues titles

If you are interested in researching further the issues raised in *Bullying*, you may want to read the following titles in the **Issues** series as they contain additional relevant articles:

- Vol. 127 *Eating Disorders* (ISBN 1 86168 366 9)

- Vol. 125 *Understanding Depression* (ISBN 1 86168 364 2)

- Vol. 123 *Young People and Health* (ISBN 1 86168 362 6)

- Vol. 117 *Self-Esteem and Body Image* (ISBN 1 86168 350 2)

- Vol. 115 *Racial Discrimination* (ISBN 1 86168 348 0)

- Vol. 112 *Women, Men and Equality* (ISBN 1 86168 345 6)

- Vol. 108 *Domestic Violence* (ISBN 1 86168 328 6)

- Vol. 107 *Work Issues* (ISBN 1 86168 327 8)

- Vol. 104 *Our Internet Society* (ISBN 1 86168 324 3)

- Vol. 101 *Sexuality and Discrimination* (ISBN 1 86168 315 4)

- Vol. 100 *Stress and Anxiety* (ISBN 1 86168 314 6)

- Vol. 91 *Disability Issues* (ISBN 1 86168 292 1)

- Vol. 77 *Self-inflicted Violence* (ISBN 1 86168 266 2)

For more information about these titles, visit our website at www.independence.co.uk/publicationslist

## Useful organisations

You may find the websites of the following organisations useful for further research:

- Amicus: www.dignityatwork.org

- The Andrea Adams Trust: www.banbullyingatwork.com

- The Anti-Bullying Alliance: www.anti-bullyingalliance.org

- The Anti-Bullying Network: www.antibullying.net

- Beat Bullying: www.beatbullying.org

- The British Psychological Society: www.bps.org.uk

- ChildLine: www.childline.org.uk

- The Department for Work and Pensions: www.dwp.gov.uk

- Digital Opinion: www.digitalopinion.co.uk

- Kidscape: www.kidscape.org.uk

- Mind: www.mind.org.uk

- NCH and Tesco Mobile: www.stoptextbully.com

- The Office for National Statistics: www.statistics.gov.uk

- Parentline Plus: www.parentlineplus.org.uk

- TheSite: www.thesite.org

- Trades Union Congress (TUC): www.worksmart.org.uk

# ACKNOWLEDGEMENTS

The publisher is grateful for permission to reproduce the following material.

While every care has been taken to trace and acknowledge copyright, the publisher tenders its apology for any accidental infringement or where copyright has proved untraceable. The publisher would be pleased to come to a suitable arrangement in any such case with the rightful owner.

## Chapter One: Bullying and Young People

*Bullying*, © ChildLine, *Are you being bullied by other pupils in school?*, © ChildLine, *Homophobic bullying*, © The Anti-Bullying Network, *What is racist bullying?*, © Kidscape, *Beat bullying*, © TheSite.org, *Don't blame the bullies!*, © 2006 Associated Newspapers Ltd, *Bullying in schools*, © Anti-Bullying Alliance, *Understanding the bully*, © iVillage UK, *Rise of the brat-bully*, © 2006 Associated Newspapers Ltd, *Are you bullying someone?*, © ChildLine, *Important facts and figures*, © Beat Bullying, *Back to bullying?*, © ChildLine, *Helping friends beat bullying*, © TheSite.org, *Two out of three teenage agirls admit to bullying*, © Guardian Newspapers Ltd 2006, *Girls and bullying*, © Parentline Plus, *Victims of bullying rarely ask for help*, © British Psychological Society, *Bullying 'affects almost every child in Britain'*, © 2006 Associated Newspapers Ltd, *Anger management skills*, © Brunel University.

## Chapter Two: Cyberbullying

*What is online bullying?*, © BECTA, *Playground bullies move into cyberspace*, © British Psychological Society, *Cyberbullying*, © Kidscape, *Putting 'U' in the picture*, © NCH and Tesco Mobile, *stoptextbully top ten tips*, © NCH, *Mobile phone bullying*, © NCH, *Concern over rise of 'happy slapping' craze*, © Guardian Newspapers Ltd 2006.

## Chapter Three: Workplace Bullying

*Bullying at work*, © TheSite.org, *How to deal with bullying at work*, © Mind, *Workplace bullying*, © TUC, *If you're being bullied*, © Andrea Adams Trust, *National workplace bullying survey*, © Digital Opinion, *Are you a bully?*, © Amicus, *Bullying: a big problem for small businesses?*, © British Psychological Society, *The bully at work: Jan's story*, © iVillage UK, *Mental toughness helps resist bullying*, © British Psychological Society, *Fear and loathing in the workplace*, © Guardian Newspapers Ltd 2006.

## Photographs and illustrations:

Pages 8, 15, 24: Don Hatcher; pages 4, 17, 36: Angelo Madrid; pages 9, 21, 35, 39: Simon Kneebone; pages 13, 27: Bev Aisbett.

Craig Donnellan
Cambridge
September, 2006